976

£5

KHY

MY FATHER'S HOUSE

MY FATHER'S
HOUSE

BY

PAULINE NEVILLE

HAMISH HAMILTON
LONDON

First published in Great Britain, January 1969
by Hamish Hamilton Ltd.
90 Great Russell Street, London, WC1
© *1969 by Pauline Neville*
Second Impression, January 1969
Third Impression, February 1969
Fourth Impression, October 1969

SBN 241 01629 0

PRINTED IN GREAT BRITAIN BY
WESTERN PRINTING SERVICES LTD., BRISTOL

FOR
SIMON, NICHOLAS AND RHODERICK

CHAPTER ONE

FATHER'S STUDY was blue. It was the last room you came to in the house. Or, if you happened to walk into it through the french windows from the beech wood, it could be the first. But as no one ever just happened to walk into father's study from the beech wood, it remained the last room anyone came to in the house.

It was a sanctuary. A blue sanctuary.

Not so long ago my brother Jamie said to me, 'Did father's room have a colour?'

'Blue,' I replied.

'I thought so,' Jamie said.

'There was nothing blue in the room,' I reminded him. 'Nothing actually blue.'

'Books everywhere. Three walls of them. What was on the other wall?'

'A fireplace, I suppose.'

We both remembered and we thought about the fire, and the pure blue of the flame on very cold nights. And the silence in the room when we all stopped talking, except, that is, for the crackling of the beech wood as it sparked into flame.

Then we remembered father's expression as we ran into his room when we had some dispute which had to be settled.

There was one on this hot, happy, summer occasion.

'Well,' said father, unwinding the glasses from off his nose and marking the book he was reading with a thin strip of paper torn from the *Daily Telegraph*. 'What is it?'

I

And he gave us the quizzical, slightly amused look that always came as we entered his study.

'Fish' (that was me) 'says that your favourite authors are Tolstoy, Gibbon, Dickens and Moses. I say that Moses was not an author.' Jamie said this in the emphatic tone of voice that he used when he suspected he might be wrong.

'Who wrote the first five chapters of the Old Testament?' Father asked Jamie.

'Moses,' Jamie replied.

'Well?'

'But it has never been proved.'

'Whoever did write the first five chapters of the Old Testament, be he called Moses, or what, he had a lively grasp of his subject.'

'All right,' Jamie conceded, 'is Moses one of your favourite authors?'

'Shall I say that he is one of the men in history who interests me most.'

It may have been because they were in the same line of business, matters relating to God, that father especially appreciated the genius of Moses. Or, it may have been that as a rather late starter himself he could not help admiring someone who did not get into his full stride until he was about eighty.

Father had told us that Moses was the founder of our religion in that he had conceived of the idea of a one God, (instead of the many that existed in Egypt at the time) and the God that existed for Moses had a healthy respect for the man who had brought him into existence. Father thought that the conversations between God and Moses were very good indeed.

'But eighty is a bit late to get started,' Jamie had protested.

'It is believed that Moses did not die until he was one hundred and twenty, and between the ages of eighty and one hundred and twenty much can be achieved,' father had said with a smile.

Once Jamie got on to a track, he was not easily diverted.

'Would you say that Tolstoy, Gibbon, Dickens and Moses are your favourite authors?'

'They were all men of vision, they all thought ahead of their time, they were all liberal, and they were all literate.' And that was all we were going to get out of father on that subject. But as a subject it stuck in my mind because for the rest of my life I have been unable to get it out of my head, that liberal is the only way to vote.

Any problem under the sun, or under the moon, could be taken into father's study. Father always had time for discussion. And he was always prepared to convene in matters of importance concerning either Jamie or myself.

Possibly one of the reasons why we have come to think of father's study as blue is because the atmosphere produced by father in there gave a clarity of vision. And blue is a colour of clarity. Early on in life we were taught that thinking with the mind and thinking with the emotions produce two entirely different results. Neither of us has managed it very well, but we know what father meant.

Now that we are grown up, Jamie and I have tried to establish our own 'blue' rooms but it has not been very successful because we have only a little of the clarity and vision.

On this same occasion, Jamie and I had another problem which we wanted to put to father, but father anticipated it by saying, 'There won't be any worry about entertaining your guests when they come tomorrow. They are all coming because they want to.'

It was not often that father forced us to entertain, because he knew that, unlike him, we were anti-social. But father was an Irishman of considerable wit and intellect and he was also a Church of Scotland minister, and this was a combination that was irresistible to both father and the parishioners.

'If only father were not Irish,' Jamie would muse, 'we could live here in a state of ecclesiastical isolation befitting all Scottish manses. It is because he is Irish that people flock in and out of here all the time.'

'It is because he is father' I said.

3

'Well, anyway, they don't get into this room,' we re-assured each other.

Jamie asked most of the questions in our family. And if they were questions about father he usually put them to me. He did not put them to our mother because she was a beautiful and artistic person whom we all protected and loved. We tried not to take too many of our problems to mother because she was already over concerned with our happiness and our health. We have gone on protecting her ever since, but now in later years we have learnt to under-stand that, in her own gentle way, she has always been a worldly woman.

One day, Jamie asked me, 'Why do you think the parents came to live in Scotland?'

'Probably because one was English and the other was Irish and Scotland seemed the obvious answer,' I suggested.

If we had bothered to find out then, this is what we would have discovered.

Father was the youngest of seven brothers, the sons of a reasonably prosperous ship-owner in Northern Ireland. If father, as an Irishman, had been the seventh son of a seventh son he would have had the necessary qualifications to be described as someone with 'second sight'. The Irish would have said, witch or wizard, or leprechaun or fairy. But in a way father was a wizard, and he was certainly a man of vision. In time he became a man of God, and if it weren't for the fact that father disliked that expression very much, we could have settled for that.

Just before our grandfather died, he said to our grand-mother, 'Put James into the Church. I believe it is where he belongs. Besides which, he might do it some good.' Grand-mother had thought it a frivolous remark, but then she was not a humorist.

At the time of grandfather's death, James, our father, was just about to burst out of his small public school in Ireland. He was an energetic boy of sixteen with an original mind and an enthusiasm for life which somewhat baffled his easy-going Irish masters.

4

'You father's last wish was for you to go into the Church,' our grandmother told James.

And surprisingly, James told our grandmother that the idea was a good one. 'Even so, I can't stand the expression, "going into the Church",' he said. 'It's as if you are shutting the door on life. Heavy oak shutting behind you.'

Grandmother may not have been a humorous woman but she was an observant one. She knew a little of life, and she knew something of her son, and when she said, 'No one will ever shut you in,' she proved to be right.

Father did not go into the Church, he simply took the Church outside with him.

He sailed through his seven years at Queens College, Belfast without any academic problems. He also rowed and played rugger for his College, and he excelled himself at amateur dramatics. 'An excellent grounding for the pulpit' was his sensible and true comment.

'Now for Scotland' he told his mother.

'Why?' she asked.

'Because it fires my imagination.'

I WILL LIFT UP MINE EYES UNTO THE HILLS. It's easy to see what must have been in father's mind.

When father first went to Scotland the beautiful county of Dunbarton was presided over by a giant amongst men called the Rev. W. H. Macleod. The Reverend Macleod, who was the son of Sir George Macleod, and a nephew of the 'Great Norman' had his actual living in the parish of Buchanan. It was from Buchanan that father was ordained by the Presbytery of Dunbarton. His first appointment was to act as assistant to Mr Macleod, and in particular to take charge of the spiritual oversight of the workmen engaged in the Glasgow water scheme at Loch Arklet and Loch Katrine.

The Reverend Macleod was a busy man with far-reaching interests and it had been his wish that he would get an assistant with an agile mind and an energetic nature. This is what he got, and the energy and enthusiasm with which father went about his tasks dumbfounded the steady Scots and caused the minister to wonder if it was man or machine that had come amongst them. But he soon found out that contained within the small, wiry frame was a needle sharp brain and a mind capable of removing the padding that makes it difficult for one man to communicate with another.

And in the quiet evenings when the Reverend Macleod and father were alone together, Macleod discovered that his assistant was also a poet.

Father settled quickly to his job amongst the workmen at Loch Katrine and Loch Arklet. And soon it became apparent that the men were being taught to fish, appreciate their surroundings and, in some cases, read books. It made no difference to father whether he communicated with them in their working background, in the Parish Church, or amongst the hills. Although, for choice, it was probably amongst the hills.

As well as being a good preacher, Mr Macleod was a good teacher, and, amongst other things, he taught father that clergyman's robes are not things to hide behind. First and foremost, clergymen are men, and after that disciples of Christ. This was not a new idea to father, but it helped to strengthen his own views about what he should do in the next war when it came.

About a year after father's arrival in the county of Dunbarton, a pebble was dropped into the glass surface of the cool waters of Loch Lomond and by the time the last ripple had caressed the heather shores, the sound of marching feet was to be heard vibrating up through the subterranean depths.

When the bugles blew announcing the Kaiser's German war, cloaks, robes, and dog collars were cast aside in favour of the khaki drill belonging to the Belfast O.T.C. The manhood of Britain had been summoned, and in answer to the call went father, not in his role as a priest, but in his nature as a man. He was commissioned a second lieutenant in the King's Own Scottish Borderers and his companions never realised that the gay Irishman amongst them, was, in fact, a Scottish minister.

Father never went back to Loch Lomond, except as a

visitor, because, by the time the war was over, he had collected mother.

When the Reverend MacLeod knew this he said, 'You
had better find a parish of your own now boy. Try Galloway,
it's a lovely part.'

So father tried Galloway and got for a parish the beautiful
part of Scotland where my brother and I were born and
brought up. Mother came into father's life when she was
doing temporary V.A.D. work in London. She worked in
what was known as the Russian Hospital for Officers. But
there was nothing Russian about the very sick Irish major
who was handed over to her halfway through the war.
Father was wounded in the head at Arras, in 1917 and when
he was brought to the Russian Hospital in South Audley
Street, the ward sister said to mother, 'Nurse Kingsford, you
will be allotted to Room 6 for the next few days as there is a
severe head wound case in there.'

At the time of mother's entry into father's life, he was
unable to see her due to the bandages covering his head.
Day and night, beauty and ugliness were all the same to him.

Nurse Kingsford went to meet her fate, carrying a tray
of medical necessities and a heart full of infinite sympathy and
understanding. The figure in the bed did not respond to
any of this, and least of all to the charm that was mother's
most marked characteristic. At that time father was very ill
indeed, and, later on, we all learnt that when he was ill,
which was practically never, he required only two things.
A warm bed, and a book. Illnesses, his own that is, were
regarded as a distortion of living and something that should
not be imposed on others.

Retreating gently out of the room, mother said, 'Is there
anything else you need?'

An almost completely submerged voice under layers of
facial bandages came out at her, 'Only that you get out of
here and leave me alone.'

An extremely un-Christian attitude thought mother two
months later when she discovered that her special invalid
was a clergyman.

7

When father's bandages were removed and he was able to see his nurse standing in front of him he said to himself 'They should have told me what she was like.'

What was mother like?

She was tall and honey-coloured, and she glowed from within. At that time she looked out on life through a hideous pair of glasses, and when the glasses were removed the impact was something very great indeed. The glasses seemed to divide mother from the world, and according to her sister, our very funny, auburn-haired aunt, she wore them for protection. As the years went by father managed to remove those glasses from mother's mind, but physically she was forced to wear them for the rest of her life. When she got older, and eyes alter as you get older, she had to remove them in order to see things close at hand. The strange, battered and yet innocent look that people have when they take off constantly worn glasses gives the rest of the world a sense of both guilt and wonder. Mother's eyes were very beautiful without her glasses and especially so because in seeing her you knew that she could not see you.

Father saw through the glasses immediately and he saw what was behind. He fell in love with it then and for the rest of his life.

During father's convalescence he began to court mother seriously. And, whereas in the early stages of their meeting he had merely indulged in the sort of flattery and attention that comes all too easily from the Irish, now he got down to the hard core of winning her.

Mother found father an entertaining companion but what she did not find so amusing was this joke about him being a clergyman.

'Prove it,' she said.

So father sent home to Ireland for a photograph of himself in graduation robes, and the transformation made mother wonder if people were right about the Irish being fey.

'Live in a Scottish manse,' mother protested. 'Impossible, my mother will never believe any of this. You had better come and tell her for yourself,' because to mother the idea of a

8

Scottish manse was just about as foreign and remote as a Tibetan monastery.

Our English grandmother was a completely erect woman. At no stage in our association with her, which, of course, all came later, were we tempted, and certainly never permitted, to call her 'grannie'. Her husband had been dead many years and having embraced within her own erect body all the aspects and attitudes of joint parenthood, she had learnt to control her children with double reins. She seldom approved of any of the young men brought home by either my mother or her sister, and the sister, particularly, was given to producing what grandmother called, 'eccentric men'. But when she heard that mother was bringing home an Irish clergyman for inspection she hardly bothered to be at home to vet this particular specimen.

'It is a preposterous suggestion,' grandmother said and in the first place she had meant that it was preposterous to have an Irishman for a clergyman, and in the second that it was even more remote to contemplate marrying such a being.

Father's imagination enabled him to conjure up the type of person who would be waiting for him in the Regents Park house. He had no illusions about himself as a prospective suitor. He was not a catch. The fact that he could give mother more in the way of love and understanding and awareness of life than any other man she had ever met, or probably would meet, was not something that would be immediately apparent to a prospective mother-in-law.

Father arrived at the family house equipped for battle. He wore one remaining bandage round his head, partly, my brother and I have often suspected, to enhance the distressed charm of his condition. Almost certainly he did not need to wear it, but if it could prove a weapon in the strategic battle between prospective mother-in-law and prospective son-in-law then, why not? As it happened, the bandage was unnecessary, or so it seemed in the face of the union of these two completely different personalities. But if the personalities were different, the interests were not.

Grandmother had strong literary interests and much of

9

this was encouraged by her cousins, the famous Mudies of Mudies Library.

Everyone in the family was a little afraid of the Mudies because the Mudies were clever. Their library was the first of its kind, and in its day unique. It provided the Mudies with a life of great stimulation and interest because it was run more as a club than as a business. Many of the great writers of the day used it as a meeting place, and a visit to Mudies would conjure up the prospect of a pleasant hour spent in literary chat and the eventual departure with beauti-fully bound leather books.

Great (great great to us) Uncle Charles Mudie had started the library, the care of which was handed on to Great Uncle Arthur Mudie who remained sphinx-like in a large office at the back of the building. But the gentle and courteous man who did most of the receiving was our grandfather. It was his pleasure to receive both the writers and the readers, and it was a life's interest exactly suited to his temperament. Unfortunately the life itself was cut short.

'Why did grandfather die so young?' I asked mother once.

'He died of a broken heart,' she told me, and we all blamed *The Times* for this.

Mudies was known as Mudies Select Lending Library, and it was that and nothing else. *The Times* (according to its name) came along in opposition to Mudies and set up THE TIMES BOOK CLUB. But it was far from select and what is more they SOLD books. They sold them in cheap editions along with bric-a-brac to catch the eye. At first, as was typical of the Mudies, they refused to acknowledge the existence of *The Times*. But as time went on they were compelled to accept the fact that *The Times* was putting them out of business.

Mudies refused to lower their standard. And these standards had been high if at times a little eccentric. The Mudie sisters, Arthur Mudie's sisters, were more than just a little in love with Italy, and everything Italian. In their view both cul-turally and romantically it had no equal. Their obsession went to the extent that they referred to their other brother,

Charles, as Carlo, and they gave high-pitched, sharp orders to their Cockney servants in Italian. Each summer they sped across the continent in a coach and six and took a palazzio on the slopes above Florence.

They went on living as if there was plenty of money, and when *The Times* had seen to it that there was no more coming in, the working members of Mudies had to be got rid of. It was our grandfather's job to sack the old retainers. These were men who had been with the firm since boy-hood and they knew of no other way of life. It broke the heart of the man who had to do it.

Mother told us that in the whole of her life with her father she had never heard him utter an angry word. He was adored by his colleagues and by those who worked for him, and because they trusted him, he found it an almost im-possible task to tell them that Mudies was to be no more. Shortly after grandfather's heart broke it also ceased to beat.

When mother brought father to meet the Mudies she was amused to find that he could hold his own. By the time Jamie and I came to know them, only the old aunts remained. They all lived together in Hornton Court, Kensington, and there was a church-like feeling when it came time for a visit. The aunts all sat in a row, on high-backed chairs, flicking witty statements at each other and making reference to books that we had not got the ability to read. Heather and haggis and broad Scots jokes from the Manse kitchen had no place in this Kensington drawing-room. As we got older we learnt to admire and appreciate them, but until the day of their death, we stood in awe of them.

When father brought mother to Galloway in May 1919 it was difficult for her to realise that she was arriving in one of the beauty spots of Scotland. She came to it in a blizzard of sleet and snow.

'You can't have snow in May' mother protested.

And father had to explain to her that in Scotland you can have anything at any time.

We don't know, but we suspect, that father was proud

of this performance put on by his adopted country. At any rate it enabled him to melt both the snow and the bleakness by showing mother what he had to show her the morning after their arrival. Mother looked out of their bedroom window and saw the River Dee curve slowly towards the Galloway hills. And when she saw the soft light on those rounded domes she forgot about the bleakness of the evening before, and she forgot that once upon a time, there had been a horror of the idea of a Scottish manse. Thereafter it never was a Scottish manse. It was our father's house.

CHAPTER TWO

JAMIE WAS born first, and from his behaviour during the first year of his life you might have thought that it was he, and not mother, who had an objection to his Scottish surroundings. He screamed his way through 365 days and nights.

Jamie has grown into a silent man, and we attribute this to the fact that he got all the desire to impress others out of his system early on in life.

Father always had a keen sense of justice and during the 'screaming' period he took his turn at walking the floor at night. In a way, he admired Jamie's efforts at disturbing the household at a time when he was most in need of support. Father could imagine that the long, silent hours must be trying to an infant who felt alone, sleepless, and rather foolish bundled up in all those shawls.

Father had no understanding of baby talk. You were born a person and remained one, in varying degrees of aware-ness, all your life. All humanity was to be respected, however small.

In the place of baby talk father used the words of the psalms. In the heavy silence of midnight, when the areas of darkness acted as a sponge to all other sounds, there could be heard the rolling grandeur of those musical poems.

'The Lord is my shepherd', that seemed suitable for a child. 'I shall not want. He maketh me to lie down in green pastures: He leadeth me beside the still waters.' Still waters and green pastures. Endlessly beautiful and serene. A message of great tranquillity, and not so very far removed

13

from the serenity of a blue study that was to come to Jamie later.

At the same moment that father discovered that the magnitude of the psalms silenced the child, the child discovered that by paying the price of listening to them, he got attention. He may even have liked it. It is almost certain that his subconscious did.

Mother and father were too poor to afford much help. Father's stipend was £240 a year which, even for those days, was an insult amongst men of learning. A little support from the grandparental homes kept the hungry wolf away from our particular manse, although the same could not be said of many others. Mother and father started with a maid and a half, and the half helped mother with the children. Father did not think it right that the half should floor-pace every night, so that is how he came to be singing into the dawn.

I arrived three years after Jamie, and by that time the joke, if it had ever been one, was over. I was given the treatment that all babies deserve, and if anyone had to pay the price on this occasion it was Jamie. It was he who was sent to entertain me when I became especially vocal and annoying.

As a result of this, we developed a strong relationship early on in life, and for a good many years after Jamie regarded me as belonging to him. There was nothing sloppy about it, he was very tough with me, literally never allowing me to cry. He set the pattern for my behaviour, so much so that when I was compelled to mix with girls, I had not got the least idea how to treat them. They never seemed to want to climb trees or 'dirt track' round the house on bicycles. I don't think I was a tomboy, it was not as studied as that, it was all completely natural.

We lived a surprisingly free life in this marvellous, rambling house, called the Manse. Nothing from the outside world affected us very much, because, for Jamie and me, most of our activities stemmed from, and had their existence in, the imagination.

The grounds around our house were exciting and extensive. We had the type of garden that was untrammelled by designs or conventions. Mother, who was responsible for the garden, had the same type of relationship with it as an artist would have with his palette. She liked to plant things in the places where they would be least expected, and her main objective was to produce colour, lots of it, for as long as possible. The garden was full of surprises and where you would expect to find a smooth lawn and a well-developed border, you would find a wilderness of exciting weeds.

But it was the beech trees which interested us most. Seeing who could climb highest amongst them was one of the things which occupied our minds. In the Manse grounds there were many ancient and beautiful beech trees, and looking at them, as we have done since, we can see that they are almost unclimbable. But when you are young, and have faith, and imagination you can climb almost anything. And if you scratch the memory even further, you can remember the things which you did that you know, now, to be impossible.

'Watch me Jamie, I am going to fly.' I was halfway up a beech tree, on about the twenty-first branch, and I was going to fly across to one of the neighbouring trees. Jamie didn't try to stop me because he wanted to find out if I could. He couldn't be sure about it.

The thick bed of moss under the beech wood saved my life, and gave us our first lesson in the understanding that human beings never cut the umbilical cord from mother earth.

We both had bicycles, fairly rickety, and not very smart, but in our minds we saw ourselves on Icarus wings. We used them for dirt track racing on top of the wall which surrounded the kitchen garden. And as the top of the wall was only slightly wider than the width of the wheel, bicycling had to be very accurate and very fast. The scars we carry on our knees today are an indication that we did not always succeed, although, once again, memory tells us that we were triumphant in perpetual motion.

We had few toys and in particular I disliked dolls. All except for Jessie. Jessie was a person and because she entered

15

into the spirit of things she was accepted between us. She was operated on fairly regularly and on several occasions had her scalp removed. Her hair, which had been an unnatural red straw was replaced finally, by a magnificent mane of dried seaweed and moss. The only time she went out in her pram was when she was accompanying the cat or the cat's kittens.

Everyone in the family loved cats, which was as well because our cook (or so-called) bred them in one of the outbuildings.

'You can't breed cats,' people would say to us. 'It is the sort of thing they take care of themselves.'

But Mrs McSkimming, the cook, did breed them. She never allowed Moffat, our cat, to have more than one suitor. We don't know how she stopped the others, but she did. As a result Moffat and her 'husband' became very attached to each other and they had regular families at the command of Mrs McSkimming.

We know that Moffat would not have done this unless she had wanted to. Cats belong essentially to themselves. They are independent, self-contained and very courageous. When they are pleased they make a wonderful noise that no human can imitate, and when they make love they produce a sound which no human would want to imitate.

I suppose that it was from the cats that Jamie and I got our basic knowledge of sex. Nothing about it ever surprised us after this. The lack of bashfulness shown by Moffat was something we found surprising in others when our time came.

Moffat would make her mate wait for it for a whole afternoon, by playing 'hard to get' all round the house. She was really very unpleasant to him and we could never understand why they stood facing each other for minutes at a time with bared teeth. Every now and again Moffat would do something positive like making a grab for him and biting. Nevertheless, Moffat was not without her own cat sensibilities because the actual marriage bed was in a fixed part of the garden. It was on one of mother's small surprising little lawns, and you came on it as you walked down a path

16

and round some rhododendron bushes. Moffat and her husband were secure in this lawn and the thick green grass must have acted as a smoothing sponge to the fierce animal activities.

When Jamie and I were in the kitchen with Mrs Mc-Skimming and the maid, and possibly the half, we discussed Moffat's sex life using the words that conjured up precisely what they were doing. It was real kitchen talk, and was the kind of language that would not have been accepted in the Kensington drawing room.

Mother's position in the household was the most clearly defined, because, to an extent, her personality was the most constant. She was always there, and nearly always in the same frame of mind. Whatever her hidden stresses might be they never became apparent to us. In any case, we tried to see that she would not have many of them because we knew that she was something special and something a little frail. She did not consider herself to be a particularly interesting person and she had no form of conceit. She was shy and retiring and this may be why her two great hobbies were music and gardening. It is possible that within those two worlds she found all the beauty and all the peace that is necessary. Besides, had she been asked, and she never was, we know that she would have said that living with father provided enough excitement for anyone.

Father spent a great deal of time flattering and teasing mother and she was never entirely certain of his humour. The Irish are not always easy to understand because it is difficult for others to realise that any race can be so devoted to their own humour. Where jokes were concerned father was always his own best audience. But the laughter was infectious. Whatever it was about father's humour the fact remained that it kept mother young and pretty and she loved the attention.

Jamie and I grew up thinking that married couples courted each other all through their lives. As we got older we were amazed to discover that this was seldom the case. When mother agreed to marry father, she had said to him,

'I shall be no good at doing churchwork, people frighten me too much,' and father had answered, 'I am choosing a wife and not a curate.'

Nevertheless, mother did get involved in parish matters, because the parish were not prepared to leave her out of it. She was necessary to them. So long as mother was present at these local meetings there was peace because she was the sort of person in front of whom people did not row. In time she became president of the Women's Rural Institute, and president of the Woman's Guild. She did it all with much grace and charm, and providing we kept away when she was making speeches she could just manage that side of it as well.

We think that speech-making took far more out of mother than father ever realized. It was an aspect of public life that held no alarm for him. Training for the pulpit is a good grounding for all forms of public address and because father had no idea of self-consciousness, he did not suffer from a fear of being conspicuous. Mother hated to be conspicuous and as time went on, and father went more into public life, she was manoeuvred into a position that she would never have chosen for herself.

To a certain extent, mother's understanding of human nature was more acute than father's. Because he wanted so much for mankind, and was so concerned with its advancement, his ideals could be let down from time to time. Mother expected little of people and was, in consequence, understanding of all their short-comings. This was a necessary balance to father's outlook on life, and if he were able to say so today, he would say that he would only have been half the man he was without mother.

There was a gentleness about mother that appealed to the toughest members of the community, and they tended to protect her from each other. She was regarded as something fragile and fine, and therefore sufficiently impartial to be arbitrator in local dispute. Father was the High Court Judge and his word was law. Above which there was the Heavenly Court and God.

18

CHAPTER THREE

ONE OF the things we liked about where we lived
was the feeling that it existed there for itself, and for
nothing else. It was the county of Kirkcudbrightshire, fertile, beautiful and self-sufficient. Anyone who came
to Kirkcudbrightshire did so because they had planned it.
No one just happened to be passing through as it was about
as far from the centre of things as the left hand is from the
spinal column.

'Kir-coo-bri-shurr' is the local pronunciation of the name
and, said like that, it has a melodious, flowing sound. Most
of the sounds round us were melodious, but they were not
always flowing.

We were surrounded by 'cchs' because as well as the
local accents, the lochs all ended in it. Our English relatives
gave it a hard sound so that it became 'lock' and to Jamie
and me this 'lock' destroyed our image of the beautiful areas
of water known as 'law-cchs'.

We were surrounded by lochs, with names like Loch
Doon, Loch Trool, Loch Macaterick, and they were all
places of beauty. But the one we liked best, because we were
proud of it, was a thin, winding, rather ugly little loch
without any attempt at grandeur, but which had the audacity
to be called Loch Auchenrioch.

By the time you had got through the Law-cch-au-cchhen-
ri-occhh, you had reached the end of the loch because it was
not much bigger than the word.

Our own particular village fitted into the mood of all
this, because it was called Claremichael, but pronounced
'Claremickel.'

Our house, The Manse, was perched on a hill over-looking the village and the connection was by a narrow drive that wound under the railway bridge, up a steep hill and through a beech wood. The village consisted of one wide street on either side of which were immaculately clean, stone, whitewashed houses. The gardens were all at the back, so that, from the one main street, the village looked like a photograph in the snow.

There were two shops in the village, and one was good for liquorice allsorts, and the other for boiled sweets. Every Saturday morning, all the children of the village came, pennies in hand, to buy sweets from whichever shop they favoured. Both Jamie and I favoured the liquorice allsorts shop, possibly because of the 'ping' on the door.

Because we always went to this shop, and never the other, we developed a kind of bogey about the second.

The man inside it frightened us a little because he had the type of wry humour that children fail to understand.

'Why don't we go in and ask for a grown-up type of thing? He will be nicer to us then,' Jamie suggested, most of the suggestions came from him. We thought hard and decided on Robin Starch. It seemed a very grown-up sophisticated kind of thing. In any case, it came most readily to our minds because the maids were always boiling it up in our huge washers, and we liked to see the large white sheets hang from the line, and flap in violent opposition to the feeling of stiffness that always began to envelop them.

'He won't have any starch,' I said to Jamie. 'And then we will be left buying his horrid sweets.'

We thought about it for years, and it never occurred to us to think of anything else but starch, and as we were certain he would never have it, we never went in.

But we think that we must have stood outside his shop discussing the daring adventure because when Jamie became 21, he received a box of starch from an anonymous giver. Long before that we had become friendly with the shop-keeper but he did not insult us by referring to our childish fears. He merely had the last little wry dig as Jamie went through the door into maturity.

One of the shops was below the fountain, and the other was above Mrs Hewitt. Everything about the village was so much the same, that the villagers developed their own distinguishing landmarks. You either lived below the fountain, or you lived above Mrs Hewitt. In the same way that when you met, you met in front of one or the other.

Both Mrs Hewitt and the fountain were at slight angles to the road, and because of this it helped to give the impression that the houses on either side belonged in a different area of the village.

Quite naturally, Jamie was the first to go to school, and he went for lessons to a Mrs Gilroy, who lived on the right side of Mrs Hewitt. Two years later I joined him there. I was not really old enough to go to school but I wanted to be with Jamie and it was thought that my presence would be unlikely to harm anyone.

Mrs Gilroy instilled into us both an acute hatred of mathematics and an undying admiration for our father. By the time we had finished with her, we regarded mathematics as being a power for evil, and father a power for good. It was a long and painful process to discover that the former conviction was innacurate. It cost our parents several years of tutoring for Jamie, and many years of humiliation for me. Even now, at forty, I still have to make rapid, silent calcu-lations on my fingers.

Mrs Gilroy had a memory that had unnerved many a good clergyman, for she went to Church every Sunday in her life, and remembered each word of every sermon ever preached. She had seen out two ministers and was now busy battling with the third.

In the end, she capitulated to the superior memory and brain of father. Every sermon of his was original and each text new. That is to say, it was new in the given context. Mrs Gilroy could not fault him, so she stopped trying.

Just occasionally, father could embarrass us by crying in the pulpit. The sad, grim, terrible things of life did not make him cry, but beauty did. And others would be amused, while we were embarrassed, to see that there were times when even his own sermons proved too much for him. He had a magnificent command of the English language and he made no secret of the fact that he knew how to put it to best effect. You cannot be in love with words without having the additional emotion of wanting to use them. Father knew when his sermons were both good and beautiful and felt no embarrassment whatsoever in the appreciation of them. This was not a question of conceit, it was a question of gratitude that such a language, with such a message, should have come into existence.

Most of what father was talking about in Church was lost upon Jamie and me because we never really learnt to concentrate there. Why should we? We got it all at home. God was a member of the family and father's way of talking about Him brought us into closer contact at home than it did in Church. But we always knew when the emotional bouts were coming, and then instead of playing with our fingers or making silent messages to each other under the pew we would look up at him with a sort of embarrassment and awe. Since that day both Jamie and I have learnt to admire the big men of courage who are able to show emotion in public.

Discussion on the subject of the Bible was always encouraged. He liked to hear our views, and one that came under discussion quite frequently was whether we preferred the beginning of the world as written in the book of Genesis or in the book of St John. This was a discussion which was particularly pertinent because we had been told that the world did not begin in this way at all. The core, the centre of father's mind was acute and factual and he had the totally, stringent, uncluttered attitude of the scientist. He knew and believed in the meaning of evolution, and early on we were instructed in it, but he was full of admiration for both the method and the beauty of the Biblical sense of creation.

Father's sermons were not always understood, but it

didn't matter because even on those occasions the congregation was aware that something extremely literate and
extremely profound was going on. The message of hope and
joy that is contained in the Bible was put to them in such a
way that if the Church had been full of frescoes they could
not have seen more vivid pictures. What is more, the parish
was proud of him because, 'clever' people came from all
over Scotland to listen to him.

You could never describe father as the great pastor. He
did not go round gathering in his 'flock', nor did he spend
much time making calls, although, on occasions he and
mother would bicycle miles into the hills to see a 'wounded'
member of the flock.

Father's attitude about people was, 'If they want me they
will come.' The manifestation of this ideal was that the door
of our house was to be left open day and night, summer and
winter, and anyone could come at any time, which they did.

On the other hand, you could say that father was a great
preacher. He would stand up in the plain, wooden pulpit,
looking out into the severe stone Church and its somewhat
severe-looking congregation, and the visions that came to
life in that Church were possible because of father's ability
to translate the Bible into a story of personal meaning for
everyone.

'In the beginning God created the Heaven and the Earth.'
Jamie preferred that because it was so visual and beautiful.

I preferred St John's: 'In the beginning was the Word
and the Word was with God, and the Word was God',
because it made me realize that before there was anything,
there was thought.

At home in the Manse, we had a pack of cards that must
have been made by some firm somewhere but in all our years
we have never seen another pack like it. I don't even remember how we played the game, but the cards, instead of
having numbers, were fifty-two representations of the great
paintings throughout history. Most vividly can I remember
a piece from the Sistine Chapel of God blowing life into
man. And when father read from the pulpit 'And the Lord

God formed man of dust of the ground, and breathed into his nostrils the breath of life, and man became a living soul', it had more meaning because of our game of cards. It was typical of father that he should find cards like that. He did everything he could to enhance the charm and beauty of life for us, or rather, he did everything to make us conscious of it.

We went to Church every Sunday, and the Manse pew was directly under the pulpit in the most noticeable place in Church. If Jamie and I got the giggles, which happened often, it was no good stifling them with peppermints because father, and the Church Elders, had eyes back and front of their heads.

The Church was shaped like a cross, and whereas we sat, you might say, up near the head of the cross, the Gordons and the Murdochs sat in large, boxed-in pews, in the cross's left and right hand respectively. The Gordons and the Murdochs were two of the big land-owning families in the parish, and they never came into the Church until right after everyone else was seated. Our local member of Parliament belonged to one of these families and his entry was the best performance of all. We never knew if he thought he was in the HOUSE, or whether he pretended to think he was, because he came in slowly, turning round to acknowledge the nods of his friends, and before sitting in his pew he would wipe the 'parliamentary' dust away from his seat with immaculate leather gloves. Just occasionally, when he, or they, overplayed their part and got in after father had entered the pulpit, we would look up at him, and there would be an almost imperceptible lowering of the left eyelid in our direction.

But when Mrs Murray, whose pew in the gallery commanded a good view of everything, came to Church, there was not the suggestion of a smile anywhere, and everyone sang a little louder and prayed a little harder, because Mrs Murray saw all. She was the largest land-owner, but most of her consideration went for the Black Missions. If the cottages on her own estate were not always in the condition that you would expect from a great and benevolent lady then one just had to remember that charity does not always begin at home.

Jamie was not afraid of Mrs Murray, but because he knew I was he behaved himself. Mrs Murray had a niece about my age who used to come and stay for a month each year. The first time I was asked to tea to keep her company, Mrs Murray spent her time looking at my knees and saying how unladylike they were.

'Well, they are used for climbing trees and biffing my brother,' I told her.

Mrs Murray was not used to little girls who played little boy's games, and she wrote a polite, but firm letter to my mother reminding her that 'one day your daughter will want to marry'. And it was apparent from her letter that my chances were pretty slim if my Mother did not do more about me.

'I won't have to go back next year,' was my relieved answer to all of this.

But I was wrong. The niece had liked me, and what was more she angled to see the much-talked-of brother. So with my knees powdered for the first and last time, I was at the head of our drive, with Jamie, to meet the niece when she came to tea.

Jamie decided that the niece was rather nice.

'Well, at any rate, better than you could have expected, coming from that place,' he said. But I decided that he liked her because of her name. The Lady Cynthia Scott. It all fitted in with our rapidly developing obsession about Scotland.

Possibly it was because we were not actually Scots that we held passionate and romantic views on everything to do with 'our country'. We found the Scottish names, the Scottish people, and the Scottish countryside just exactly how we wished them to be. To anyone outside the family, we were persistently boring on the subject of Scotland and we loved every minute of the superiority we felt about our Scottish obsession.

It was completely unnecessary for us to have strong Scottish accents because our parents had the sort of voices that go with an upbringing and an education not restricted to the village school. But Jamie and I developed our accents in such a way that when we were at our broadest we could be understood only by the maids in the kitchen. We took our accent on with us to boarding school in Edinburgh where the humour of the situation was not appreciated.

In time, we cultivated an in-between, half-Scottish, half-English, family language that was useful for transmitting private feelings in public places.

But it was the romance of the Scottish names that affected us most and it was the Scottish attitude to them that provided us with our greatest source of pleasure.

Referring to a man by the place he came from, rather than by his own name, was something that extended from the highest in the land to the lowest.

When one of the maids would inform us that, on her day out, she had seen Glenlaggen in Castle Douglas, it did not mean 'Birnham Wood be come to Dunsinane'. It meant that John McGaw of Glenlaggan had been in Castle Douglas doing his shopping.

Market day in Castle Douglas was a form of paradise for us because not only would the roads be impassable through sheep and cattle being driven up and down them, but in the market square itself were gathered the men who had come in from the hills, the valleys and the lochs. In huge strident tones they would yell at each other, proud possessors of their own heritage. Arrogant, uncomplicated, and absolutely without fear of anyone or anything.

'Bulgard was buying big today,' Jamie would inform father when we got home.

'I hope you don't make a nuisance of yourselves when you go into market,' our mother would wonder with her gentle concern.

'And Glenlochairn,' I would go on as if we hadn't heard mother, 'told Balwhinnoch that his cattle were a disgrace.'

'By any chance, are you two referring to Mr McKnight

26

and James Johnson,' was father's form of mild rebuke, But we knew that he loved those place names as much as we did.

He told us of a reception given in Edinburgh where all the Scottish Chieftains and their wives were assembled. When giving their names to the man who announced them, they always referred to themselves by their estates rather than by their proper names . . . i.e. Cameron called himself Lochiel, and Scott, Lochbuie, and so on. Father arrived in time to hear the famous K.C., Frank Lockwood, later knighted, have himself announced as '104 Portman Square and Mrs Lockwood'.

'When I grow up I am going to marry Macdonald of the Isles,' I told Jamie one day.

'He might not want you,' was Jamie's thoughtless reply.

'Well then, Cameron of Lochiel.'

I used to say the names over and over to myself, and then I tried fitting them to nameplaces.

Jamie decided it for me by suggesting the Kyle of Lochalsh, 'It is opposite to the Isle of Skye,' he said, 'and it may belong to Macdonald of the Isles in any case.'

Years later, we visited the Kyle of Lochalsh where people spoke in soft, lilting voices, and the sun was bright until midnight.

It was sad to have found the Kyle without Macdonald.

There was nothing soft and lilting about the voices in Kirkudbrightshire. Theirs is one of the toughest of the Scottish tongues, but it has a grandeur that fits the mood of this strange isolated country.

CHAPTER FOUR

IN OUR childhood, there were no such things as tourists. A few people came on holiday to stay with other people. But they were usually relations, and therefore belonged to the place in a borrowed sort of way. Just occasionally some entirely new-looking people would appear in our village and that would upset what Jamie and I called 'the fancy' of the place.

'Fancy' is not easy to define, but it is nothing like as whimsical as it sounds. It is really rather vicious because it can spoil everything. The nearest interpretation of it is 'mood'. But unfortunately it is seldom the mood of the person concerned that creates the fancy. It is a mood that is imposed on you by another person, or a strange happening. A strange person coming into the house could distort the fancy for days.

'I can't help feeling that it is all rather spineless,' Jamie said to me once. 'We should be strong enough to impose our own moods and feelings on things. Why should we allow other people to make this house feel and look quite different?'

I could never quite think how to answer his question, because the whole feeling was in a dimension hard to put into words. The best medium I have found for expressing it is through painting. You can paint the same thing a million times but the mood is different in each case.

It was no surprise to me that people should affect atmosphere, I expected it. They are very upsetting things, people. And it was too much to expect that they would be in accord with us.

Artists came from all over the world to paint the Kirk-cudbrightshire scene, but, somehow, it does not matter when a tourist is also an artist. Artists don't disturb nature, they pay homage to it. Even if they paint badly they are still paying homage by the very fact that they are trying to imitate, or at best, interpret it.

No one who came to Kirkcudbrightshire ever forgot the evening sky. More often than not it would be thick and luscious and looked as if blood oranges had been squeezed down over the cloud formation. These formations were so earthlike that when they hung over the Galloway hills it was impossible to sort out which was earth and which was sky. The gentle, blue-green of the hills would wilt under the violent purple and crimson from above in ecstatic submission.

Our house, which rambled off into pieces of thirteenth-century architecture, and in consequence had become almost part of nature itself, had one view of the village and another of the Galloway hills up the river. The word 'hill', in Scotland, can mean any mound stretching to about 2,000 feet. It is the kind of understatement that the Scots like to indulge in. They are not people that go in for extravagances or overstatements. As a form of praise, 'it is no baad', is about as much as you can expect.

But anyone who thinks the Scots are mean would be making a mistake, because there is a world of difference between meanness and caution. And the things that matter most to them are not talked about. To try and describe the beauty of evening over the River Dee would be an insult to nature, they would feel. It is better, therefore, to go the other way and say, 'It is no baad.' This expression has saved Jamie and me many a heartbreak. After we left Galloway, and came back on our rare visits, some scenes were too beautiful to be anything but painful. 'It is no baad', would get us out without too much anguish.

Attached to every Manse in Scotland is an area known as the glebe. In fact, it is nothing more than an ordinary field. However, it has the special privilege of being part of the Manse, and inconsequence it has a magic of its own.

Our glebe had the magic. And it was a place with an almost indestructible fancy. Contained in this field was a small wood, a rabbit hill, a marsh, and a tiny loch which was quite separate from the river.

Morning and evening brought in the ducks. And if you have ever been out at dusk, waiting for the tiny, dark silhouettes to make their appearance round a bend in the sky, because the sky bends at that moment, you will know the thrill when a 'honk honk' turns them into geese. The swish, squelch and plonk, the faint flapping and chattering that announces their arrival in the marshes, is the manifestation of all excitement produced by nature, and it is indestructible in the memory.

Shooting on our glebe was forbidden. One of the things about father was that he liked the idea of freedom for all living creatures. It also fitted into his teaching because he tried to encourage freedom of thought. If he taught discipline it was done to encourage right-thinking. It was never done as a form of imposing one will on another. Everyone must be free to think, even although at times it might be necessary to show them how to set about it.

So the fish went freely up the river, and the birds flew in to rest at night. The only sound to disturb it all would be the lapping of our boat as Jamie and I set off on one of our many all-day picnics.

We liked exploring our countryside, and every place was different from the last, and different from the last time we had called. Kirkcudbrightshire has many moods, especially when it is mirroring colours out from and back into the sky. And, above all, in the mind you can create as many mountains and rivers as you like.

At that time there were plenty of grouse on our moors, and as we walked up and away from the river, the heather which always scratched our legs also hid the possibility of finding a hen grouse on the nest. We quite often found the grouse, but we never saw their nests because at our approach they would scuttle, run or fly, squawking like tuneful hens, in an effort to discourage our pursuit.

About two miles westward through the village from our house you came to the Airds Hills. The Airds Hills were magnetic. Not many people lived amongst these hills, and so it was a matter of surprise to the parishioners that father's rather stern-looking black bicycle was often to be seen there propped against the stone dykes. They were a little more used to the sight of Jamie and me practising our skids with hands off the handle-bars wherever there was loose ground. They expected, perhaps, that we would be amongst the hills because this was where the little roads were at their most dangerous. What they did not realize was that we were often in those hills and walking far away from our bicycles.

Father taught us about the little areas of perfection in life. You can see it with the slow dropping of water from a leaf. You can see it in the crisp and isolating glitter of morning frost. You can see it in a smile that has just washed its way through tears, and you can hear it in that one particular note in music which strikes through the final defences.

With the appreciation for the small areas of joy, there follows the wider entanglements of the remote and the unseen. Whatever it was that we found amongst the Airds Hills, it is certain that we all found it. Not one has discussed it with the other, and like father's blue study it remains both a vision and an experience in the memory.

Rabbits were everywhere in those days and the hills were dotted with their burrows. Dangerous for unsuspecting ankles, but enticing for small fox terriers.

Our dog, Oats, who came on every exploration with us was more concerned with the wild life around him than the beauty of the hills. He got demented with excitement, but was altogether too confused to do anything but run from one rabbit hole to another, shouting with pleasure.

Oats was the only person in our family who could make father walk. Father was not a walker. He was a thinker, a reader, a talker and a listener. Father did not like walking except for Oats, and here was a tyranny that father did accept. He was amused by the strong-willed determination of his dog because it had come about as a result of the very

31

freedom that he allowed it. He appreciated the irony in this, and he loved Oats.

Each morning after prayers, for we had prayers in father's study when breakfast was over, Oats would come into the study and sit in front of father's armchair. He would then out-stare father. It didn't matter who called, or what else was going on, Oats sat. Eventually, father would recognize the inevitable defeat and, getting onto his feet, he would say, simply, 'rabbits'.

With an excited yelp, Oats would lead him out onto the glebe. And there they would go, these two solitary figures separate from each other because father could never maintain the pace, and yet absolutely together. Even when Oats was old and father more disinclined, the charade went on.

Occasionally something would happen to frustrate Oats' plan, and mostly it was when father would get involved with a visitor and Oats would be asked to leave the room. But Oats saw to it that these visits were curtailed to their minimum.

In the rather wide hall outside father's study there was a huge red leather sofa onto which were thrown all the things that had no immediate purpose. Amongst others, there were usually balls, varying from rubber for Oats, and tennis for me, to rugger for Jamie. Oats' plan was cleverly thought out, and had anyone ever really wanted to stop him from carrying it out (which he did often) we would have removed the balls.

Oats would push one of the tennis, or rugger, balls under the sofa, and then go after it. The sofa was low on the ground, and inevitably Oats would get stuck, which is what he wanted. Thereafter, he would pretend to be a fox terrier down a rabbit hole, and the yelps, screams and barks that resounded round the house were sufficiently graphic to drive out what to Oats were unpleasant and unwelcome visitors.

Most mornings were without interruption, and once on to the Glebe, father and Oats would make for Rabbit Hill where the rabbits were in their legion. In all the years that we had him, Oats never caught one rabbit. We don't believe that he really minded, although we felt that just one, to prove himself a fox terrier, might have satisfied honour. The relationship between father and Oats was so close that it seems possible that father managed to transmit to Oats the idea that the chase is all right, but that the kill is not. It would seem unlikely that this idea could defy nature. But you cannot be certain.

Father knew that certain things had to be killed to keep the cycle of life going. Each animal lives off another, and in the general scheme of things man lives off cattle and sheep. Father would have preferred that it wasn't so, but as he was not a vegetarian, he went with the scheme. What he would not countenance was man intervening out of turn. And for this reason he would not allow anyone to interfere with his Rabbit Hill. Oats did not kill the rabbits, so he was damned if he was going to have the farmers come with their guns.

There was another department of our private animal connection which caused some of the surrounding farmers a great deal of annoyance.

Just at the head of our drive, before you turned the corner to be confronted by the house, there was a magnificent cathedral of beech trees. They were tall and very thick at the top, with elegant overlapping branches. Every year rooks came to build their nests in this beech haven. And every year the farmers came to protest about the damage done by the rooks to their crops. In particular, there was one farm across the river from us that received the main impact of the damage. After a time, the farmer stopped coming to see father about it, but for some years he made us an annual visit. Father was always very polite to him, thanked him for coming, but always ended up by saying the same thing.

'But it is so very loyal of the rooks to go and do it in another parish.' He really thought that they were very clever rooks. Eventually, the farmers would come when they knew father was away, and then they would take few shots at the rookery. They thinned them out a bit, but it was difficult to relieve a country of such a well-founded dynasty. So the rooks con-tinued with their grating caw, their bad manners to other

33

parishes, and the possession of our drive. Their droppings painted the drive below and, every now and again, one large splash would land on a forgetful head.

Jamie and I loved the rook chorus. It was the forerunner and rearguard noise to everything that happened at the Manse. The rooks sensed the dramatic, and were a party to each whim and change of action that occurred. Rising in black discordant clouds above the trees, they announced the arrival, or departure, of anyone on the drive.

CHAPTER FIVE

IT WOULD be difficult to say at what moment father decided to go into public life, as opposed to public service. We think there were two reasons for it. One was because public life decided they needed father, and the other that something to do with it made father angry. Indirectly, I caused the anger because I was ill for a year, and during that time the inefficiency of hospital services was shown up.

One night I was struck with a blinding headache, and the following morning I was covered in spots. The headache is still with me as a memory, because it was the first thing that happened to me that was really frightening. Mother was always a sympathetic and kindly nurse, but the one thing that she could not do was take away the fear.

Once the spots had revealed themselves, Dr Fortune was called in. And when he diagnosed measles, a hush descended on the house, and the curtains were drawn. Measles was a very serious illness then, and I had it as badly as it is possible to have it.

Everyone loved Dr Fortune because he minded so desperately about his patients. It was generally agreed that he should never have taken up medicine as a profession, but it was also agreed, that there was no doctor like him. He did not seem to know a great deal about the human body. But he had great reserves of knowledge about the human mind.

Dr Fortune and father were friends. But it was a friendship that had the appearance of two satellites revolving round each other. Friends demand things. Father and Dr Fortune made no demands. It was an association rather than a friendship. And it was the type of relationship that each required, exactly.

Dr Fortune could do very little for my physical wellbeing, but as time went on he could, and did, do much more for the other side of my nature.

To begin with, my temperature went up a little further each day. And when it was as high as a thermometer can register I was packed in ice and everyone held their breath.

The period of delirium I can't remember, but one picture is still as clear and as delicate as a transfer on a shroud. I woke one morning and saw out of the window that the path leading down from father's study to the kitchen garden was banked with a mass of gold. Spring had come, and the life giving golden rays of the sun had painted the daffodils an imitative yellow.

'Spring,' I said, and the fever was over.

Dr Fortune was with me all through my recovery period and what he did was to take me on a voyage of discovery into the Children's Encyclopaedia. The children's stories that mother had been reading to me were not pleasing. In fact, they had an irritation. I disliked the sickly, cloying charm and morality of fairy tales that ended well, and the unreality of princes and princesses.

'It doesn't mean anything to her at the moment,' explained Dr Fortune. 'Give her facts. She has had enough fancy and fiction in the tormented world she has been living in for the last weeks.'

My bed was in mother and father's room during this illness, and the security of this helped with my recovery. But mother and father never got away from it all and when, on the very eve of my recovery from measles, I contracted Whooping cough, we became encased in a nightmare world of our own.

It was never known how I managed to get this particular illness because no one else in the house or in the village had it. I whooped on for two months with the aid of a little oxygen pump, becoming weaker and more miserable as the months went by. Spring seemed to have left me once more, and the sun and all its golden delivery was far away from the blackness and illness of my own mind. So when fate struck for the third time it was no longer a matter of speculation or wonder. It had become almost a part of living. But this time I was taken away, and that was the worst nightmare of all.

'Where is Jamie?' I asked as I was lifted into the ambulance, because I had never done anything without him before. It seemed a betrayal that he was not there and not coming with me.

During the illnesses I had not asked for Jamie, somehow he did not belong there. But the journey and the thought of what was at the end of it made me want him with the sort of longing that is total. Jamie had been sent to prep school in Moffat. It was time he was away because the shrouded atmosphere enveloping the Manse was something he neither understood nor could become part of. Father's efforts at uplifting and disengaging him from the quagmire of the illnesses helped only for a time. Eventually he was ready to go, and somehow, in his mind, it was not a desertion to be leaving a sister who had moved away from him. Father was right. Illness is a distortion of life and no one but the poor sufferer can really be a part of it.

Hatters Castle, if you know about it, will conjure up for you everything in the way of a house of fear. When I entered the scarlet fever hospital I knew fear made physically manifest.

Due to the fact that my fever had an unusual twist to it, and my mind was suffering from the residue of past illnesses, I was not put into the ordinary scarlet fever ward. I was put into an isolation ward with two cases of meningitis, because the hospital thought that I had both scarlet fever and meningitis.

All through the first night there I lived in a state of petrified silence. Everything was white, and everything was still. Ill as I was, I realized that one of the white, entirely motionless, figures was dying, and when she did, I realized that the finality was nothing compared to that silent, lonely dying.

The following night, the second patient died, and when she was taken away I was left with the empty, shadowy memory of them both.

The nurses who came into the room, spoke in whispers as if they were anticipating my departure. And when I said, 'Why?' they crushed my questions with rigid fingers held to white lips.

On the third night when I was removed from the room I thought that it must be because I was dying. Like the others, I was being taken out, a silent, motionless figure. It was only then that I wondered why I was going through it without Jamie. Although I didn't die I did make the discovery that we have to manage some things alone.

I got over that long, pale nightmare eventually but it happens that nothing in my memory is comparable to the hell of those three totally solitary days.

Father did not get over it. When he heard about the abominable blunder and incorrect diagnosis of illness, he experienced an anger that went beyond the accepted bounds of range. Looking back on it now, it is possible to understand that his anger was born out of a virulent imagination. He had been able to live through every agonized moment of my solitude, and he never quite forgave either himself, or the authorities, for permitting such a situation to come about. Father's love for us was not just a parent to child relationship, it was all of the deep feeling that any one individual can have for another human being he respects.

But it was his deep-rooted loathing for sloppy thinking and muddleheadedness that sent him into action. Stupidity amongst those who are supposed to be professional is something father could never forgive. Mistakes were permitted by the innocent, but, in father's view, those that set themselves up as knowing should know.

Within a few weeks of my recovery, father was standing for election for the County Council. It was the year 1936 when he got his seat in the Council and it was then that he started on his task of improving the health services in, first of all the county, and then in the country.

Until such time as father was given his own office in the County Buildings our nursery table was used as his official desk. There was an unspoken agreement amongst us that the study would not be used for such a purpose. The complicated network of paper and document that gathered on this table came to be known as the pyramid. Strangely enough it resembled one. Father had a way of getting documents from out of the middle of the pile which in no way upset the flat surface at the bottom or the peak at the top.

Our large, nursery table told the story, in pyramid form, of father's service in public office from 1932 until 1960. Or, at any rate, it would have told the story had anyone bothered to study it. As it was, no one did. Father never tried to bring us into that side of his life, we did not belong in it, and he had no wish that we should.

It is possible that we did not really appreciate father's importance in the country. As the years went on, his interests and activities grew to a proportion with which we could not cope. But then we were given no encouragement to regard him as a man with an official position. His position in the Church, and his place in the home, were the only facets of himself that were to concern us. But one day Jamie and I looked in the paper, it was some years after we first went to school, and saw attached to father's name, the following,

Moderator of Presbytery and Moderator of Synod,

Chairman of the Health Committee for Scotland,

President of the Association of County Councils in Scotland,

Convenor of the Stewartry of Kirkcudbright and the Lordship of Galloway.

There was a magnificent ring about this. What father actually stood for had never properly formulated in our minds. But this was a heraldry indeed, and the Scottish significance of it is what appealed to us most.

Although mother, Jamie and I did not know very much of what was going on in father's public life, we found, none the less, that to an extent, we hit the public eye. It was not that we sought it for ourselves because, due to our rather solitary existence, we were self conscious with people. But we had to admit, from time to time, that the faint halo of glory that seemed to be surrounding father was a pleasant thing to bask in when it had a connection with our beloved Scotland.

Word soon got round that father was both an accomplished and humorous speaker. As a result, he was invited all over the county, and beyond it, to open functions, or to touch off the spring of a new organization. Mostly, we managed to get out of accepting the invitations that included us, but, just occasionally, mother persuaded us to go with father.

The Scots arrange their functions to take place in the afternoon, and we think this is because of their devotion to afternoon tea. Most of the functions that father attended, were accompanied by a good tea. In the normal course of events, we hated parties. We disliked the forced gaiety that went with them, and even more, we disliked the sticky girls in pink dresses. When we went with father to some of his functions, we were left to ourselves to get on with tea, and as this was what we liked the ordeal was not too great. Mother usually stayed at home, and this we also liked because when we came home there was always someone to tell things to.

We think that one of the reasons why father liked and felt at home making speeches, was because he never saw people as a crowd. No matter how many were there, he saw them as individuals. In the same way that he managed to make his sermons to a congregation seem like discussions on a person to person basis, he made each member of his audience feel that he was talking to them. Father never saw an anonymous mass in front of him. They were all people, all different and all significant. Fortunately father was not a raconteur, the jokes he made usually sprang from an idea of the moment. Sometimes we inspired the idea.

Anyone who has suffered from a parent who public speaks will know all about the family jokes being washed in public. If Jamie or I had produced some point, or made a remark that father considered applicable, he would use it. He had a way of making us sound funnier than we were. At first we were acutely embarrassed and always wondered if the laughs were because we had smuts on our noses, holes in our clothes, or just nasty expressions on our faces. In time we developed a sophisticated veneer, which did not fool each other, but we managed to sit back with one knee carefully crossed over the other, appearing to share the joke.

Only once did we hear father be unkind. On this occasion he used his wider grasp of things to silence a woman who was persistently irritating and petty. It was a public meeting about hospital services, and this woman was reducing everything to the first person singular, as was her wont. The first person singular was something father did not care much about, and when the thin dried-up voice had been haranguing on for some minutes, father interrupted to say, 'Forget about yourself as an individual and remember that you are merely part of a process.'

The woman had not understood the remark, but the reaction of the assembled gathering was such that she was happy to sit down amongst an anonymous mass.

Later on we had a discussion with father about processes. Father regarded man as an interesting phenomenon. Quite one of the most interesting phenomena produced out of the mind of God. As such, mankind fitted with all other phenomena. In father's view, man should be a non-isolated and non-static being, and women of the type at that meeting depressed him because they represented civilization in a motionless condition. Immobility and self-complacency being dangerous to the advancement of man.

Father's way of expressing himself was not always understood. He had an original way of emphasizing a point and we think this may have been because he saw almost everything in picture form.

On one occasion the wife of one of the Church Elders telephoned mother to ask if she and father could go to dinner. Mother explained that she was unable to go and when the woman persisted by asking father alone, mother turned to father and said, 'Would you like to go alone?' 'Say to her,' father replied, 'Where would Hamlet be without the Prince of Denmark?' Mother who was a faithful recorder of father's remarks, said just that.

It took a little time for mother and father to climb back into favour with the austere minds of the very literal Elder and his wife.

All father had done was to indicate to the Elder and his wife that that he and mother were as much the same person as were Hamlet and the Prince of Denmark.

The Irish in father used to boil up occasionally and come out through a jet which was pretty forceful. The Scotsmen amongst whom he worked learnt to let it steam itself out. They learnt that it came only on rare occasions, and when it came it was usually with justification. The thing that everlastingly stands to father's credit is the fact that he lived, as an Irishman, to be a leader amongst the Scots.

Looked at squarely in the face, he was an intruder. The Scots, especially, are keen about running their own affairs, and there may have been moments when the pill, which was father, was hard to swallow. But for reasons that are a credit both to father and to those amongst whom he lived and worked father was always accepted. When he had left Loch Artlet, his first place of work in Scotland, he had received a handsome testimonial subscribed to by every workman on the site, 'irrespective of creed'. As an epitaph, I think it serves him well.

But all of this, father's public life, and its effect on us, came some years later and before it we were able to snatch from our existence at The Manse the golden years that helped so much later.

CHAPTER SIX

JAMIE'S FIRST holiday from prep school, and my resurrection from the sick bed coincided. We have never enjoyed anything so much as that first holiday when the shackles of our first real experience in life had been removed.

Father seemed to be more at home than usual, and the blue room still held all of the tranquillity that had been part of our lives before the disruptions came.

Mother's and father's bedroom was above the study, and when I was ill, but no longer delirious the knowledge of father in his study meant a great deal more to me than all the warm drinks and general coddling that went on up above. There were times when I would just lie in a vacuum, and into the nothing would come the feeling that warm thoughts were about me. I would transfer the thoughts back into the middle of father's room and very soon I would be there with him.

During that first holiday, Jamie and I did in fact spend a lot of time with father because we both had many questions to ask.

But the very first one, and the one that we needed to ask the moment we both returned was, 'Why are there sheep on our glebe?' was taken care of by Oats.

Father had been persuaded by an impoverished farmer to let him have a year's grazing for his sheep for nothing. As father could never refuse a request, the sheep came. Equally Oats was determined that they should go. Every day, he watched the sheepdog at work, and then, one day he decided to try it out for himself.

Our cook came to the study and told father that he had better get out on to the glebe to 'his' dog. Father, who never liked that tone of voice and suspected trouble when it came, did get out on to the glebe but there was absolutely no dealing with 'his' dog.

Oats in a whirling, flurrying ecstacy of delight was chasing one sheep after another into the river. In the end, the total loss was only two, but it was enough, especially for a poor farmer.

After such an incident, people expected that we would get rid of Oats, but then people had not reckoned with father. In father's way of looking at things, you did not 'get rid' of any living creature. They either died, or they met with an accident. The sheep, alas, had met with an accident. Oats on the other hand had not, so he lived.

However, Oats did get the one really severe telling-off of his life from his master. Unfortunately, Oats was not made of the stuff that is happy in adversity, so he took himself off for three weeks. For the first week of his absence we were distraught, and messages went out round the country about Oats. During the second week, father came to the accurate conclusion that Oats was all right, and that he was displaying a form of independence. During the third week we discovered him in the middle of a measles epidemic. An epidemic that father always feared I had started.

Flora Duncan, Jamie's passionate admirer in the village, went down with measles first, and after her, four more of her family got it. The Duncans lived in the smallest of the village cottages, and they were the largest family in the village. Just how many of them slept in the same room, or bed, for that matter, we never knew, but what we did know, in time, was that Oats moved in with the start of the family epidemic, and only moved out when the last child had recovered.

Oats had sworn the family to secrecy, and even though we passed their cottage continuously in our search, we would never have known of his whereabouts, had not our maid, Meg, given the show away.

Meg was unable to keep anything to herself. Not of course that she tried. She was proud of her slightly superior position as the Minister's maid, and she never could resist the temptation to report village news to the Manse, and Manse news to the village.

So when she told us that Oats 'was in bed wi the wee lassie in the Duncan's hoose', she hardly regarded it as a betrayal of a confidence because they all knew what she was and should never have told her.

After that, whenever there was an epidemic in the village, Oats left the Manse and took up residence in whatever house was afflicted at the time. It was not that Oats was punishing father by staying away as often as he did, it was just that he did so love the sweaty warmth and comfort of those beds.

Most people thought that Oats was given too much freedom, and that for a dog from the Manse, he was badly behaved. They were right of course, except for one thing. By having so much freedom, Oats gave a great deal of happiness to a great many people. He was, after all, a big character, and the children in the village adored him. Furthermore father believed that animals were your friends and not your slaves.

Quite a number of people thought that Meg was given too much freedom for a Manse maid. And, of course, they were right about that too. But then Meg had been born free and would die free. She was born out of free love, believed in it herself, and taught both Jamie and me that love could be many things but that mostly it was fun. Everything was fun to Meg, she adored life, but there was one ceremony that used to wipe the smile from off her face.

In our village it was considered to be putting on 'side' to get married in Church. Getting married in Church was left to the farmers and other more elevated members of the community. Therefore, a quiet service down at the Manse was what the village families liked and what they got. Jamie and I were present at these ceremonies whenever possible, because we liked to watch the funereal expressions on the faces of, what we considered must be the victims.

We knew nearly everyone in the parish by sight, if not by name, and for the rest of the year we had a friendly relationship with them all. Come the day of the wedding, both blood and expression seemed to drain from their faces, and they looked at us if we could have been stone images standing against an ancient wall.

We loved to watch Meg's face which was a picture of rapture, but also despair, and we never knew if it was because of what she was missing, or because of what she feared might be coming to her.

Father wore all his robes on these occasions, and by doing so managed to give the parishioners the impression that the vows they were embarking upon were as sacred within the four walls of a house as they would be in a Church.

Meg always opened the door to the couples. Mother stood inside the first hall to welcome them, and then Jamie and I would adorn the second hall and approach to father's study with grinning faces and friendly hands. Finally the couple would enter father's study where father would be waiting, prayer book in hand to receive them into the sanctity of marriage.

After they had gone in mother would come up to us with an anxious face and say, 'Did you notice if father had remembered to change his handkerchief?' and then we would all have to escape to the sitting-room where we would laugh.

Father had no consciousness of his own appearance. He was without conceit of any kind. He was not interested in his own clothes and positively disliked anything new. He had an old and trusted relationship with the two suits that he possessed, and although he was aware that cleanliness came next to godliness, he was not all that happy about his suits going to the cleaners. The mirror in his dressing-room was cracked, so he must have spent years looking at a distorted vision of himself, and the one downstairs in the cloak-room was yellow with age. It is doubtful if he really knew what he looked like. I don't believe he spent much time wondering if people liked him, and most certainly he gave no thought to their views on his appearance.

He was not a handsome man because he was too small. And I suppose his head was too large for his body. We never remember him as anything but bald, but when he put on his large, black, flat, clergyman's hat, he looked about twenty-five. In fact, at the time that we became really conscious of him he was forty-six.

If a point had to be made about father, one that would last as an impression and would be easily recognizable, it would be to comment on his youthfulness. It was not the bouncing, gay sort, it was the alive, always interested kind. He was an extremely attractive man whose facial expressions were so numerous that strangers coming to the house used to think that there were many more of us than there were.

We all took turns to dress father before he went out because we could not rely on him to do it properly for himself. He never noticed if his socks matched and if the shoes were a pair. He had one old pair of leather gloves that sat at the end of his fingers, and a scarf that wrapped round his neck so many times that his head became more formidable than ever.

When mother asked if he had changed his handkerchief, it was a metaphorical appeal to us to assure her that everything was in its proper place. It was also a genuine concern about father's handkerchief.

Years before, father had seen the agonized expression on mother's face when pulling his handkerchief out of his pocket in the pulpit, he realized how dirty it was. He had taken it out to flick off some of the dust that the ancient Beadle had been too blind to see. Having dusted the pulpit with an already partially grey handkerchief, he then started on an attack of sneezing which often followed the arrival of dust, pollen and the like.

Mother had to sit through nearly ten minutes of this act, and it was only at the very end that father realized that a hush had fallen on the house, and that waves of sympathy were going out to protect the scarlet cheeks on mother's face.

On most occasions after that, mother saw to it that father's handkerchief was changed. But sometimes she forgot, and when father had been cleaning out the henhouse, bathing Oats or tinkering with his old car, which we hated, just before going to Church, the handkerchief with the whole story written on it would be brandished from the pulpit. Jamie and I know that this one little quirk was the nearest father ever came to sadistic thinking. He enjoyed the joke about the handkerchief and he enjoyed mother's embarrassment.

In the same way that father was not interested in any form of self-decoration, he was disinterested in possessions. He was almost completely non-acquisitive, and if anyone gave him a present he would hand it over to us without even opening it. There was just one thing about which he was almost greedy. Books. He was a voracious reader. Everyone gave him books for Christmas, because they knew that nothing else would be appreciated. The study walls were lined with them, and there was a certain order of priority about where they were put. As the years went on, the order went, and the house resigned itself to an elegant disarray of books which were as varied in content as they were in cover design.

Among some of his other activities, father took on the Chairmanship of the Library Committee. This became one of his few indulgences. It also enabled Kirkcudbright-shire to have a better lending library than they would other-wise have known. Most of the new books that came into the main County Library were vetted by father, and the ones of paramount interest found their way into a small, brown leather briefcase which, in its turn, found its way to father's study. He never came home with less than four at a time. Father maintained that there were four moods in a man's nature. That is to say, there were four headings, with many subsidiaries underneath. The categories were like this. En-quiring. Requesting. Receiving. Disbelieving. In the first category came all the books of a technical, or professional nature. They were to be read for the exclusive purpose of finding something out. Next came those that fitted a need of an emotional nature. It could be about art. It could be about love. At any rate, it was to fill the emotional hungers. The receiving books were the ones that came at you just because of themselves and not because you had need of them. Lastly came the books that were read as a form of dope. They were not to be believed, or believed in. They were fantasies, fairy tales, and they were the escape when needed.

Father liked to read all the books first. If any one of us got at a book first, it spoilt it for him.

He loved the idea that a completely new book had come into the library and the first person to read it was himself. This was an indulgence we never denied him. He had so few wishes and wants, and this seemed a childishness, and a human weakness that brought him nearer the rest of us.

When father started me on the first volume of Gibbon's *Decline and Fall of the Roman Empire*, I was too young to understand about his four categories. I have wondered since into which category my reading of this was supposed to come. It is almost certain that it was not the enquiring one, because I was too young to take it in. Jamie and I have decided since that father left out a fifth category which seemed, and seems obvious to us, although, it is possible that, to him it was such a basic necessity in all categories that it need not be mentioned. The category, of course, is literature. The *Decline and Fall* is a great literary achievement, and I recognized it, the language that is, when I first read Winston Churchill. Running currently with Gibbon, I was given John Buchan to read because he represented the gay challenging side of life. Jamie, before me, had been given the same treatment, and he, like me, was taken to the places in Galloway mentioned in *The Thirty-nine Steps*.

'If we get through the *Decline and Fall*, we might be taken to Rome,' Jamie suggested, and I believe if we had stuck at the volumes this is what would have happened. As it was, we never read more than one each.

Father encouraged us to read about the discoveries of the great philosopher scientists like Galileo, Newton, Darwin and through to Einstein. By reading these, our view of God and everything that existed in God could have been shattered.

As it was, because of father's attitude in these matters, and reading them as young as we did, the Cosmos and God fitted together. That the creation of matter might have come from a blinding explosion of energy, that the approach to the origin of life might lie through a hypothesis of spontaneous generation, in no way upset our idea of the Garden of Eden. In the first place, we did not and were not expected to believe in the Garden of Eden. In the second place, even if we had, a scientific explanation did not knock the idea of God on the head. Father thought ahead of his time because, as a clergyman, he included in his thinking the Mathematical Universe as well as the Heavens.

'All things are possible,' we were told and we believed it. Father was convinced that ours was the greatest age yet, because, amongst other things, men were beginning to understand about the genius of God.

'Now that the great mathematicians are being accepted as men of genius and not cranks, the riddle of the Universe is beginning to unfold. Take Einstein, he, and a few of his colleagues have produced the greatest achievement of the mind so far.'

'Will his equation change the world?' Jamie asked.

'It has already changed man's understanding of it. At the same time, through this discovery, Einstein may release a power in nature so mighty that man will be in the position to use it for his salvation or total annihilation. God's purpose is that it shall be for the salvation of man, and not the destruction.'

Our struggling attempts to understand Einstein were rewarded inasmuch as we liked what he had to say on the subject of relativity. We liked his question, 'Where does the observer stand when he observes anything?' And we liked the answer which was, 'Man, the observer, is part of that which is being observed.'

This meant that when watching the heavens, we were a part of them.

This was one of the most satisfactory discoveries of our childhood. This and the realization that all things are related to each other. This conception gave me great happiness when, later, I was discovering about the unity of things in painting. In time, our interest in Einstein helped to change our views about mathematics. It did not alter our ability, but it stopped us thinking that Pythagoras was the sort of person who should have been taken up on to Mount Olympus and sacrificed to the gods.

Father tried to stop us from thinking of God as a being with a limited brain like our own. 'Throughout history the genius of each age has added a little towards the under' standing of a mind capable of everything.'

'But what is the point of it all?' Jamie asked.

'The study of what you call "the point of it all" is what keeps man alive,' father said. 'The development of the mind towards the understanding of the Divine Purpose embraces all the sciences that exist. As yet we have only penetrated through the first layers of understanding.'

'Illustrate,' I said to father because he always did and would.

'Take the ant,' father said. 'When you tread on it, do you think that it has any conception of the leg above the foot that has trodden on it, or further do you think it has any understanding of the body and the mind that controls the body that is behind the leg that is behind the foot that trod on it?'

'I don't find statements like that make God any easier to believe in,' Jamie said.

Why do you expect it to be easy?' father asked. 'The easy thing is to disbelieve. Anyone can do that. Anyone at all. Believing is faith, and it is very difficult to have faith. It is putting your trust in something you cannot prove.'

'Then why do it?' Jamie asked.

Because it works,' father replied. 'The people with faith are the happiest. Look around and you will see for yourself. Christianity works, when people follow its true meaning.'

'What is its true meaning?' we both persisted.

'Love. You see, it really does drive out fear. And it is fear that corrupts and corrodes people. They can't trust their neighbours so they kill them. Hit first, think afterwards.

'When these great men of science look through their telescopes out into the moving, and possibly expanding universe and see all the miracles of creation, it is merely another way of magnifying God. That is to say, it magnifies His genius, His greatness. He produced the home of life out of His genius, and all He asks is for us to keep it going by feeding it with love.'

'I don't like the hymn, "God is working His purpose out, as year succeeds to year",' Jamie told father, 'it gives the impression that He does not know what He is about. It looks as if He is trying to get it right but hasn't yet succeeded.'

Father did not mind this type of question. It would have seemed impertinent had it come out of context. But coming into the type of discussion that so often took place in father's study, it was accepted as nothing more than a view, or a genuine enquiry.

'Don't forget,' father answered Jamie, 'that hymns are written by people like us who are questing after the truth, and the words of this particular hymn come from a man who held his view about the point of creation, in the same way that others held theirs. You could argue that God had His purpose mapped out before the world went into existence, or you could argue that the purpose was being worked out all the time.'

'I think he ought to have known what He was doing right from the start,' Jamie said.

'Both the men of religion and the men of science think He did,' father replied.

Jamie and I grew up thinking of God as a genius, and as yet no one has entirely disproved it.

CHAPTER SEVEN

TWO YEARS after Jamie's departure for prep school, I joined him in Edinburgh at a school called St Trinians.

It is unnecessary to give any space to the description of that school. It has been done by a man whose ability with a drawing pencil will exceed for all time any effort that could come from the pen.

Unfortunately for me, our grandmother chose our schools, and she chose them because she was paying the fees. At the time when she interviewed St Trinians, the headmistress was away, and grandmother was lulled into a state of euphoria by the second headmistress. The second headmistress had a very gentle exterior and, alas for me, it fooled grand-mother.

At nine, I departed for school, and it is next in line to the scarlet fever hospital for black memories in my life.

I was sent away because all the illnesses had made me introspective and tiresome, and more or less unmanageable when Jamie was away.

I returned home the first holidays with all the spunk, and all the life, taken out of me, and it was only when Jamie came back that I returned to life.

But it was during those first holidays that I set about imprinting on my mind certain things that were vital to me if I were to return to this school of black memory.

One day I said to Jamie, 'When you are at school and have nothing to do, what do you think about, Fish?' because we called each other 'Fish'.

53

'Home' he replied.

'Yes, but what sort of things about home?'

'I get pictures out of my mind,' he told me. 'They are stored up in there,' he said pointing to his head, 'I store them during the hols.'

'I must do the same thing,' I told him. 'And next hols we'll swop pictures. We might even have a few of the same.'

After I learnt to do this, never again did I see the Manse as a whole. It was different little floating particles of brilliance that fixed themselves to the forefront of my mind and the house became divided into sections of pictorial memory.

Daylight in our house came in through our parent's bedroom, and went out through mine. During the day, the whole house was brilliant with light, and even on rainy days, the light from the sunny days before kept the house in a glow.

Each morning seems like the creation of life once again, and up there, in those Galloway hills, the awakening is new and fresh and divine. Birds usually bring the day into existence, and if you live near a river you will hear the river echo the calls almost before they have been made. It is as if the river brings the sounds forward from the night so that they may not be lost into oblivion and forgotten in the long stretches of eternity. For the noises at night are very different.

The friendly call of the plover turns to a more discordant 'pee-wit, pee-wit' as it scratches lines of distress against the night sky. And the curlew whose haunting, watery call saddens even the daytime, brings further distress at night. Perhaps it is the geese, flying in perfect formation, honk-honk-honking their entrance to our marshy part of the river, that give the feeling of security which helps to unite the night and day. For theirs is a solid arrival as they come down with a sort of pink precision onto strong but strangely delicate feet.

People told us that we were lucky to live in a wild fowl sanctuary. Hints were dropped to father about an invitation to shoot. But there was never any response from him because he felt that if people must kill the lovely, wild birds, then they must do it anywhere except on his land.

Bird and animal lovers were very acceptable in our house. Killers, never.

'Don't get the idea that your father is a cissy,' our artist uncle, Archibald Thorburn, told us. 'He has probably got more moral fibre and guts than most. His handling of people, and his great war record, prove that.'

I don't believe that Jamie and I ever thought of him as cissy. In fact, we had a healthy fear of our father, and had he been the least bit soft this would not have existed. However, we liked to hear anything Uncle Archie had to say on the subject of father, because we very much loved and respected Uncle Archie.

Archibald Thorburn's paintings of birds, and all wild life, are probably the most accurate and the most feeling in existence. This came about as a result of his being both a brilliant draughtsman and a dedicated observer of nature. He loved his subjects, and would go to the final lengths of discomfort and inconvenience to himself to find out if the right-hand tail feather of some bird was touched with pink or blue.

He came to stay with us quite often because we provided him with all that he required most in life. First of all, there was freedom to do as he wished. Then there was the absolute knowledge that the creatures he so loved and admired were safe. In the evening there was father to talk to. Students of nature and students of man have much in common because they have got outside themselves in the study of something else. Sometimes they would sit through the night talking, observing the stars, poring through books, illustrating points with pens, pencils, paintbrushes. Some nights Uncle Archie would stay out all night in order to catch the first light of dawn and the movement of whichever creature he was studying at the time.

One morning Jamie came down early because he had heard Oats fussing about below him in the nursery. The golden shafts of morning were only just beginning to point the way towards daylight, and as Jamie and Oats crept out of the house, a movement in a hollybush near the front door startled him. Peering up into the bush he saw Uncle Archie perched on a branch, peering with round excited eyes at the antics of a robin.

Uncle Archie came back into the house scratched and bleeding, but oblivious of all else but the fact that he had caught the angle of some particular movement of the robin.

Our river was wide and long and it acted as a boundary between many of the parishes in the county.

In all of these parishes, father had friends, but in particular he had his colleagues the other ministers.

In our view, there is no such thing, as the dour, humourless. Scottish minister. It may have been that we were lucky in father's associates, or it may be that the Scottish minister caricatured from history no longer exists.

In our experience, the ministers were all literate, charming men, whose lives were restricted only because of the miserable stipend they received.

The training to be a presbyterian minister is one of the most rigorous and exacting of all professions. During this period the acquisition of knowledge is high, and it may be that this makes for a certain eccentricity among presbyterian ministers. All that knowledge has to manifest itself in ways other than the clerical, and 'our' ministers' interests were extremely varied.

One of father's colleagues wrote beautiful little madrigals with strange poignant words. Another wrote constant letters to *The Times*, most of which were published because the prose was worth the muddled thinking contained within. Then, of course, there was father's neighbour across the water, the lean-looking silent highlander whose absorption of literary facts was almost as great as father's. Father was especially grateful that his immediate neighbour should have a library nearly as large as his own. They spent a great deal of time rowing across the river to each other equipped with the usual case of books. The parishioners on either side loved the sight of the small, wiry man with the flat hat, and the tall, rugged man with the round hat, pulling their way across the waters, far removed from the incongruity of the sight, and yet very much part of their surroundings.

The wife of this particular minister, the minister of Balheuchan was one of the few close friends that mother had up in Galloway. It was not that mother was against making friends, it was just that she did not seem to need them. Mrs McKnight did not need friends either, and perhaps this is how the relationship came about. As a result of this fairly close union between the two families, Jamie and I got drawn into an association with the three McKnight boys that we could have done without. All three of them were too clever for us. It was not that they thrust it at us, it was just that they could not help excelling in everything. They went to the same public school as Jamie in Edinburgh and when Jamie came home for the holidays he did not want to see any more of them.

Ian, the middle son, was a good shot. He used to rise early in the morning, and we would hear a shot ring out through the dawn, and we would know that another bird had fallen. The one redeeming thing about this boy and his morning massacre was that he was always accurate.

'Don't blame him too much,' Uncle Archie would say to us. 'He is a master of his art, and that is something.'

'Is killing an art?' I asked.

'The killing side of it does not come into his mind. What comes into his mind is the thrill at his own accuracy. It is also a battle of wits. One false move and the bird knows that you are there. It is a great study as well as everything else.'

'Uncle Archie,' Jamie said one day, 'have you ever shot anything?'

'No. I should never want to do that.'

But we noticed that he was very far from blind to the needs and interests of others who did.

'Father,' I said one day, 'it is strange that people who shoot are nearly always wild life lovers. It does not make sense to me.' Father smiled, 'It takes a long time to learn that you know nothing. Always remember this. You know

57

nothing, nothing at all. If you always remember this, you will never judge people. It is not for us to do the judging.'

When does a man learn humility, Jamie and I have often wondered. We knew that father had it, and we knew that he had courage. At any rate we learned about it as time went on, because certain aspects of his public life were bound to come home to us. We heard about 'the cleansing of the Temple' that went on in the Council buildings. We also heard about father's oratory when the authorities wanted to stand by the systems as they had always been, and father wanted to have them changed. In time we came to see a little of all of this in print, because each week the local paper and eventually the Scottish papers, would report father's speeches in full.

Father probably reached the peak of his oratory powers when he became Convenor of the county sometime in the late forties. By this time he was never referred to as anything but the Convenor, and judging by the way that some of the Councillors talked to him in Council it is obvious that they had forgotten that he was a clergyman.

That was the way father wanted it to be. There was to be no softening of the punches, and there was to be no ecclesiastical veil drawn over proceedings. He was there, sitting in his emblem of the Church, and people had to learn how to reconcile this with the other side of things. This worked, because, to father there was only one side of anything. The workable side. God was not apart from anything he, or they, did. He was the Grand Designer behind it all, and father was lucky enough to be a particularly articulate instrument in God's hands.

No one was embarrassed by father. The 'dog collar' was there, but they spoke to it as they would have spoken to a collar and tie. As a result man met man in the council, and the only superiority that father had, although did not feel, was one of intellectual ability. They respected him in council, but they hit him hard when he needed it because, as everyone knows, idealists can be unreasonable people.

What is a Convenor? Those who lived outside Scotland

would ask. We never found an answer to this question because no one in Scotland ever attempted to explain it. It is not comparable to anything else because nothing else describes it. If you are a good Convenor then you hold a position that is untouchable and unquestionable. You are referred to as 'The Convenor' and whatever you say goes. You are the father of a very large family and you are the head of a very important house. If you are a bad Convenor you don't exist.

At any rate the Stewartry of Kirkcudbright knew their Convenor. One day father's car was stolen, and the indignation round the county was surprising. Father had parked the car in its usual rather too far from the curb place, outside the council buildings in Kirkcudbright. When father came out the car was gone. Being father, he did not consider theft and, in fact, none of the councillors did. Father's car was very well known, and the number plate SW 6060 was a sort of by-word.

Father was convinced that he must have parked the car elsewhere, so he and a County Clerk walked the streets looking for it The County Clerk rang the police and said,

'Did you take the Convenor's car?'

The police said they had not taken the car, but much more of his type of parking and they would. The County Clerk was not amused at the time, but when he told father what the police had said, father saw the point. Father wasn't a selfish driver, he wasn't even a thoughtless driver, he was simply a driver who never thought about driving. As he drove along the road his mind would be engaged with varying subjects, and when he came to park the car he would still be thinking about them. We are not quite certain how he survived on the road and on one occasion both he and we nearly did not.

We were on our way in this funny, nameless, rickety car to Glasgow to see the pantomime. The roads were icy and we should not have been on them, but we had a date in Glasgow and father intended that we should keep it. Half-way there, we came round the corner and went into a skid on black ice. Jamie and I were slumped in the back of the car, reading the same book, and did not notice what was going on until we heard our mother say, 'James whatever are you doing?'

James was trying to stop the car from hurtling from one side of the road to the other and when he did not manage to achieve this, the car shot up a bank on the side of the road and turned completely upside down.

In those days windows opened only halfway down and if the car doors got jammed, it was almost certain that you were not going to get out. On this occasion the car doors jammed, the engine caught fire, and the windows opened half-way down.

Mother was wearing a heavy fur coat given to her by her own mother and in our anxiety we forgot to take it off her. Jamie and I were concerned that mother should get out of the car first, and we started to push her and her coat out through the half-way window. In the end she fell out onto her head and bruised her face. Jamie and I followed together because that was the way we did things. And last came father. We got out just before the car exploded. If Jamie and I had been a little more charitable we would not have found ourselves with the immediate reaction, 'Thank God that's gone.'

After about five minutes when we all had time to think what had happened, reaction set in. Mother started to shake and I shed some of the few tears of my childhood. Jamie decided to be a man like father, and when father said that we would go on to Glasgow in the first transport that came along the road, Jamie said, 'Good idea.'

None of us wanted to go but when the large bus came slowly down the road on that black ice we found ourselves being pushed into it by father. We don't remember anything about the pantomime and if we do its tucked somewhere in the subconscious, because it was about giants and evil spirits, and it comes back to us in sleep as does the journey on that road to Glasgow.

Sometime later, I heard father say to mother, 'If we had

not got them onto the bus that day they might have been nervous ever to go in a car again. It really was a very good move going to Glasgow.' We know that mother didn't agree, because she had looked white and terrified the whole way there and I think that when they got into their bedroom in our hotel that night, mother and father came close to the only row in their marriage. Father was a very courageous man because he knew the moment, and there are only very few, when people have to be forced to do certain things.

On the day that father's car was stolen, and this was a different, and nicer car than the last, the county, and the county police searched until nine o'clock in the evening.

The police rang us at home, 'It has been found,' they said.

'Where?' father asked.

'Near Carlisle,' was the reply.

'What happened?'

Apparently, the thieves had used the car for some job which took them into England. The progress of the car had been noted all the way down the main road because the Convenor's car was so well known. People were in the habit of saluting it, and when they received no answering salute they knew that something was wrong. By the time the car was near Carlisle the police were on to it because there had been so many telephone calls.

'Did you know that you had taken the Convenor's car?' the police asked the thieves.

'The wot?'

'The Convenor's car,' the police reiterated.

The thieves did not know and it is unlikely that at the time they either knew or cared what a Convenor was. But it is equally likely that they were more selective in future.

CHAPTER EIGHT

THE ONLY two people who ever attempted to interfere with father's pyramid in our nursery were Meg and Oats. Occasionally Meg would try to help father by looking for a missing document. In fact, she was looking to see if she could acquire any local gossip, Oats, on the other hand, did not even make a pretence of helping. He was there to disrupt it. It was a form of protest.

One morning father was shut in his study, with a visitor, for longer than Oats deemed either considerate or necessary. In fact, father was interviewing a doctor from Dumfries (a gynaecologist) and Oats may have considered this visitor to be an intruder.

'Right,' he said to himself, 'we shall see what we can do about this.'

In a small wood at the back of the kitchen garden there was a hole in the ground with a mossy surface. If Jamie and I had discovered the hole before Oats, it is the sort of place where we should have gone whenever we had anything secret to think about. But it was a little too small for us because it was a perfect fit for Oats.

The hole was quiet, and shaded and earthy. It was thick with smell and significance relating to all forms of nature. It was also the high altar of the more depraved side of Oats' nature.

From time to time Oats liked to roll on dead skins. If he found one that was sufficiently flavoured to suit his highly developed taste in these matters he would take it to his hole. And there he would roll on the skins until every pore in his body had absorbed the aroma coming from this highly charged object.

He would then come up to the house with a stink that would pale the efforts of a skunk, and the first person given a chance to share in this orgy of nature was father.

Father considered this to be an animal indulgence which should not be denied to Oats. He was never angry about it. Instead he used to take him down to the river where Oats would be made to swim in after sticks. It got rid of the smell, it gave father extra, and much needed, exercise and it gave Oats a double dose of attention.

On the morning of the gynaecologist Oats went too far. He brought down the curtain on that type of charade for ever. Having decided that he must get rid of the gynaecologist, he also thought that he would teach father a lesson about neglecting his, Oats', special time of the day. We are not certain why he did not resort to his usual trick of getting under the sofa outside father's study. Perhaps he had the idea that on this occasion it would not succeed.

As it was, he went down to his hole where he rolled on a piece of rabbit skin which he must have been saving up for some time and from there he came straight up to the nursery where he finished his rolling on some of father's papers.

When we realized what Oats had done, because that type of smell does not take long to penetrate through to the various extremes of the house, we waited. There really wasn't anything else to do because none of us was prepared to touch the table.

Father came out of the study with the doctor and we watched them walk through the hall to the front door, and we watched the expression on their faces as they exhaled the entire contents of their lungs. When father had said goodbye to the doctor and turned back into the house, his face was stony. He walked straight to the nursery where Oats was waiting. Oats was no coward; he knew what he had done, and he knew that it would be given either a good or bad reception. Father would regard it as a joke, or he would not. Father did not regard it as a joke, and picking

63

Oats up in his arms he carried him straight out to the wash-house, where for an hour he scrubbed him with carbolic soap in water which was just under boiling point. And when that was done he put him in the airing cupboard to dry.

'You can make up your mind,' we heard him say to Oats as he was closing the door, 'that it is an indisputable fact that carbolic soap will eclipse every smell you try to bring into this house. And another thing' we heard him add. 'I will not countenance bad manners.' From this we gathered that the performance with the ball under the sofa was decent fun whereas the recent act was not.

The biggest disaster to strike us during Jamie and my prep school years was the death of Oats. Unquestionably it hit father the hardest. I don't think any of us had realized just what Oats had meant to father. Not everyone understood father's humour because it had enough Irish in it to give an exclusiveness for just father. Father had brought Oats from Ireland and although from the time we knew him, Oats was no puppy he was, nonetheless, every bit as young as father. Oats understood father's humour, and most of the acts that he put on were for father's benefit. In the same way that quite a few done by father were put on for the benefit of Oats.

Oats made no fuss about dying. We are not even certain if he had been ill. Certainly he became frailer. And the morning walk on to the glebe with father took longer, and seemed a little more painful daily. But Oats did not appear to suffer. One morning I was sitting in the nursery in a large chair reading a book when Oats came in and climbed on to my knee. It was an unusual thing for him to do because he had always been too independent for slop. He nudged aside my book, turned round several times on my knees, and died. I did not know it was death until father came into the nursery to look for Oats. He took him off my knees, and holding him in his arms, he stood for a long time looking at him.

'You have done well, scholar, old chap,' he said finally.

Almost every child in the village came to Oats' funeral. Father was not a part of this because, for father, the end had come with Oats' death. His spirit had gone on, and father saw Oats with everlasting freedom.

But Jamie and I cared very much about Oats' physical being, because we could not separate the spirit from the body. We wanted that the whole of Oats should have a good send-off.

Jamie took the service by the side of the river, and I led the singing. When that was over, we rowed him out to the middle of the river and gave him a sailor's grave. We knew it was what he would appreciate most.

Flora Duncan came back to tea, and she and Jamie stared at each other's tear-stained, freckled faces, while I kept up a conversation which no one appreciated.

We never had another dog after Oats. It would be difficult to say exactly why we didn't. Perhaps we were protecting ourselves against another heartbreak. But I suspect it was because it would not have been fair to any other dog. No animal could have taken Oats' place. After Oats' death, Jamie and I stuck closer together than ever. While he was alive, we took our walks individually. Fundamentally we preferred, and still prefer, to walk alone. A little later on, but for a short time only, I learnt what it was to walk with someone else. The addition of Oats was merely an extension of oneself, in that he fitted the mood exactly. So, for choice, Jamie and I took it in turns to go for the big walks with Oats.

For a time after Oats' death, Jamie and I went everywhere together. On the whole, we liked doing the same things, and certainly we liked the same places.

Possibly our favourite walk was to the farm where we collected the milk. It was three miles out of the village on the other side from us, and it was a climb uphill the whole way. We did not enjoy the climb, but the farm itself seemed to be on top of the world, and the run down was worth the climb up.

When we were little, we walked to the farm, swinging

the large milk can between us, and singing songs to the rhythm of our footsteps. As we got older, having acquired bicycles, we went on those. We raced to the farmhouse and came to a skidding halt outside the sweet warmth of a byre full of Ayrshire cows.

The farmer's daughters always came out to greet us, and there were huge grins spread across their polished red faces. They laughed at everything we said, except when Jamie got carried away with the thought of his own humour and started to make jokes on purpose. Then the broad grins faded into surprised little mouth-shaped rounds.

We never managed to milk the cows successfully. We tried often, and Jamie took it seriously, but I found it a slippery, slightly hysterical occupation and was thankful when the cow rebelled.

We were a little afraid of the farmer because he was a small man with a dour character and a large voice. When he said 'Good morning', everything in the farmyard started to scuttle. He shouted at you when you were standing right beside him, and the echoes of his voice round the farmyard drowned your answer.

When he died, which he did when we were still quite young, we felt that the voice might have had something to do with it, but we were sorry that we hadn't liked him more. After his death, his wife took on the voice, so that we felt her days would be numbered too. Which, strangely enough, they were.

When we bicycled home, there was usually a small trail of milk drops on the road behind us because we raced at top speed down the hill, and because the lid of the can did not fit properly.

We had used the same can as long as we could remember, and the idea of acquiring a new one never occurred to anyone. The can had a special place in the back kitchen on a small shelf, beside the bowls that were kept for the cats.

Moffat was the only one of our cats who had a place in our household. She came to Oats' funeral, whereas her

66

progeny were too busy off after their own carnal pursuits to bother with such a thing. Moffat was entirely black except for the tip of the right ear which was white. It was a very sensitive ear and it shook when Moffat talked to us. It was not that Moffat talked much, and when she did it was usually about herself. She protested if her routine or her comfort was upset in any way. That is why we were surprised when she came to the funeral. We had not realized that she cared for much else beside herself, her home and, possibly, the cook. Looking back on it, we think Moffat must have had some kind of deeprooted, traditional respect for Oats who, as an animal, had about the same sense of independence as Moffat. When Oats was alive, they paid no attention to each other. On the other hand, there was a feeling of vacuum when one or the other was missing.

Strangely enough, we don't remember when Moffat died. We are not certain if she did. At any rate, not at the Manse. We are inclined to believe that she took herself off to some quiet place, and in her own neat and fastidious way gave up what by then was probably the struggle for living.

Jamie and I spent more time in the kitchen than either mother or father realized. Our cook, who was a staunch member of the Women's Rural Institute, was always trying out new W.R.I. recipes on us. But there was more to it than just the recipes, for Mrs McSkimming's language would have sent the Church Elders into an early grave, had they heard it. Furthermore, a lifetime of hobnobbing with the men who came in vans delivering meat, groceries, vegetables and fish had given her a fund of stories that made conversation about as unnecessary as a drop of water into the ocean.

Once or twice, Jamie gave the show away by repeating in the dining-room some of the stories he was too unselfish to keep to himself. A great deal of the time, we did not really understand what they were all about. But Jamie was able to reproduce Mrs McSkimming's voice to the life's image, and the tittering, giggling, sucking-in of teeth that

67

went with the story told father all too well that this one was not suitable for the Manse dining-room.

The punishment was never very severe, for father was much too full of admiration for the performance in general to concentrate on the details of what the story was about. In any case, he was never very good at interpreting broad Scots.

CHAPTER NINE

I WILL LIFT UP MINE EYES UNTO THE HILLS FROM WHENCE
COMETH MY HELP.

And from whence cometh some of my inspiration. That,
at any rate is what we felt about father.

The clarity of vision that comes from hill-gazing and the
inspiration that follows, is something that can best be understood by those who have done it. Mountaineers will tell
you that the spirit of the mountain does not reveal itself
to you until you are on the mountain itself.

As non-professional mountain climbers, Jamie and I
found that the view looking down from a mountain is not
to be compared with the one looking up. There is a magnificent and dramatic sense of the impossible about mountains
seen in the distance, and the fact that a spirit, or spirits, live
there can be a surprise to no one. To a certain extent climbing
them shatters the illusions because the exquisite vision turns
into earth and stone. Not being a keen walker, father never
attempted to climb the Galloway Hills, and for him they
remained a remote and slightly divine image, but whose
base was carved out of the substance and beauty of nature.

The words of the 121st psalm appealed to father because
of their poetry and because of their meaning. It appealed
so much that we had to restrain him from having them
sung each Sunday in Church.

'You can't have it all the time,' we protested. And
sometimes father would look a little sad at that but would
continue instead his silent communion with the hills.

The communication that exists between nature and man,

69

exists most strongly when the man in question has a little of what can best be described as magic.

It is my belief that the world is made-up of human beings and super human beings. Some of the super human beings may not necessarily accomplish anything very spectacular but, nonetheless, they do belong to what can be described either as the Inner Circle or the Outer Circle. They are all in touch with something that is above 'ground level', and their very existence in this life enhances things for others.

People who came to see us at the Manse knew within a short period of being in the house that magic existed there. Not all of them understood where it came from because, as a result of being part of the Manse, a little of the magic washed off onto every member. Even the animals had it, and to a lesser extent, so did the maids. We were all brushed with a thin coating, but we knew that it stemmed from father.

It was not something that was ever discussed. Put into words, it would have sounded both ridiculous and, in the circumstances, possibly a little irreligious. The idea being that you cannot have wizards and witches for clergy-folk. But, the truth is, that the Great and the Enlightened through-out history have been a little bewitched.

In the Centre is the Magician in Chief, or, otherwise God. Close to him in the perimeter come the superior interpretators like Aristotle, Plato, Homer, Leonardo, Rem-brandt, and from these, it extends through various stages to the outer ring where the magicians are possibly less creative but equally enthusiastic about trying to understand and then explain the meaning of life.

Father found it exciting to be alive because he felt it a privilege to be part of such a magnificent construction. His joy was trying to explain this to others. The unspoken idea was that he as an articulate member of the Magic Circle was in a position to explain to the world, but in particular to his congregation, that the gift of life was indeed a gift. But, and this was the most important aspect of father's magic because it had the most effect on the lives of others, he was a practical man when it came to the actual business of living. Father knew that men could not appreciate the existence of the Divine Spark, if they were sick, ill-clothed, ill-fed and ill-educated. And so, because he was a clever man as well as being a slightly inspired one, he became what it was necessary for him to become, an administrator. And as an administrator he was able to see to it that his own people, at least, were housed, educated and generally looked after.

It never was suggested, and it never will be, that father was a saint, or that, even remotely, he resembled a saintly figure.

Thank God for it. It would be impossible to live with a saint. It would be like having a beam of light in the house showing up the dust in every corner.

Father was no saint, and, like all positive men, he was disliked by some. But even his harshest critics had to admit that when dealing with him their time was never wasted. It was always possible to get straight through to him. He did not surround himself with padding of any sort, either mental or physical.

His office in the County buildings, the Convenor's office, was like a monk's cell. And it was like a monk's cell because father chose to have it that way. If you walked into it on any one day, you would think it had just been vacated. There was a desk in the middle of the room. And on the desk there were two pencils, two pens and one telephone. The telephone was seldom in use because, we believe that, fundamentally, father mistrusted the telephone as a form of communication. According to him it distorted not only the voice but the meaning contained within it.

Father would sit in the middle of his room, in the middle of his thoughts, making-up his mind about what was to be done concerning the matter in hand. He seldom referred to notes because the majority of his filing system was in his head. His memory was something with which most people did not try to argue. In the first place, he had a photographic mind and could commit whole pages to memory after the first time of reading. And in the second place, he had a multiple pigeon hole filing cabinet in the back of his brain. Facts went in, in their right order, and remained there, ready to be brought into conscious use at any time.

Only recently, I was trying to impress father about how far back memory could go and I said,

'Lord Salisbury claims that he can remember being born.'

'It was Lord Melbourne,' came the immediate reply.

You could not beat him, because he was unable to forget anything. This ability did not irritate us but it may have maddened some of his colleagues. It was not that father was trying to score points, it was simply that he loved accuracy.

Even although father's memory was incomparable we don't think that even he could have had more of the sense memory than is ours today.

Probably each person could have a chapter in their lives devoted to pure sensation, and when Jamie and I look back on those early years at the Manse we think we are remembering them through the senses. Or, perhaps it would be more accurate to say that we feel we are remembering them through the senses. At any rate, one of the things that can do it today is the vibration of a tennis ball hitting the racquet.

Jamie and I always acted as ball-boys for father's tennis games, because father's serve was rather like his bowling in cricket. It was hard and high and very often bounced off the back line and up over the net at the back of the court.

Usually Jamie and I went with bare feet on those occasions because the contrast between the velvet padded court and the prickly, jagged grass around it helped to intensify the excitement of the game. We always wanted, and expected, father to win, and as he usually did we had the satisfaction of being the children of one of the best tennis players in the county.

Steamy sweat, related to thick white sweaters, established on tartan rugs, thrown over green painted iron seats, tucked under rhododendron bushes, gave to the game the restful end of several hours hard labour. And above the heads of the spectators, the rich, lush, fruity petals of deep pink rhododendron flowers, gave out their opiate smell, and silenced the relentless search of the bees.

Sucking the sweet juicy texture of the water from young grass, Jamie and I used to watch Oats make tunnels through the rhododendron leaves. He went in to the bushes backwards, and came out the other side frontwards, and sometimes with a rhododendron petal balanced on his nose. It was a joke. He was pretending to look for rabbits. It was a hot, midsummer, sweet-smelling joke. It was also a way of distracting father from pursuing something that slightly irritated Oats.

Oats knew that chasing tennis balls was not approved of by father. In his, Oats', view, all balls were things to be chased and for this reason he thought it inconsiderate of father to keep him out of the game for so long.

Usually, the long juicy grass came out of its holder with a smooth and satisfactory division. At other times, it snapped halfway, and then the taste was more bitter, and the texture rougher. Sometimes 'Cuckoo Spit' would appear on the bit you wanted but we didn't mind that, because we loved the cuckoo and believed it to have spat there.

The call? cry? song? moan? appeal of a cuckoo is still one of the most poignant and sensation-giving noises to be heard in nature. It brings in the summer, and even if the day is grey and damp, the cuckoo call manages to superimpose on it all the luminosity of a sunbaked summer scene. It never surprised us that the cuckoo did not have time to build its own nest. And we felt delighted for the bird who was lucky enough to be chosen as a foster parent to the young cuckoo. For the cuckoo, with its strange haunting sound, is busy keeping up the continuity from one year to the next. When you first hear it, in early summer, you can recognize the call from the year before. You can hear it as it goes back, and echoes back, and back from one summer to the one behind it. It is as much a part of our countryside as the drums are of Africa.

Towards the end of the tennis match, Jamie and I would

walk down to the kitchen garden to pick the strawberries and the raspberries for tea. We knew that the old gardener, Bob, would be there picking them before us, but it was almost unbelievably magical to walk in to the kitchen garden when Bob was there because Bob talked to his garden and made everything come alive. Growth in it had an illogical pattern of behaviour, because, defying all the laws of nature, the things Bob liked best grew best. And the failures were punished, because they were not cherished and nourished like the others. Happily for us, Bob, Jamie and I liked the same things.

Bob stank. There is no other word for it. But it was a stink you could cope with out in the kitchen garden. It had to be called a stink because it was too strong to be called anything else. It was arrived at through several factors. One was that the windows in his cottage were never opened. After that it was affected by the animals that lived in it with him. Bob preferred animals to people. He wore an old cloth cap day and night, we were sure, and he gardened with his hands and never with a spade, shovel or fork. Oats and Bob did not get on, which was a surprise because Bob gave out the sort of smell that Oats could not have thought up on his own. We think that Oats resented the fact that Bob was such a character. It may have been professional jealousy, because they both competed to be first with father and Oats suspected that Bob came first. In fact he was wrong.

Often when we were in the kitchen garden with him, Bob would tell us the latest instalment in the saga of a family called Stuart who lived at what we called The Cross Roads. The Stuarts were always in trouble, and the daughters were wild. I was not certain what 'wild' meant, but in my mind it had something to do with our lush kitchen garden, the stink from Bob, people dashing in and out of a white cottage at a junction of a road, and Jamie's upturned enthusiastic face. We ate too many strawberries during this tale to make it possible to do justice to them in the dining-room. Even when the thick cream wedged its way over the uneven pattern of fruit in the bowl, our interest was not aroused, because it had been so much more fun stuffing ourselves in the kitchen garden with Bob.

You can't enjoy raspberries until you have picked them for yourself, and had the fun of examining the pale, velvety inside for the sight of a tiny worm. The smooth interior, with just an odd ruby sparkle transposed from the outside is a thrill to discover when it is free of a worm, or an imperfection of any sort.

'Will you have strawberries or raspberries?' was always the great question. It seemed a stupid one to us.

'I want both,' is what the guests wanted to say. But, 'whichever you have the most of,' is what they did say.

Jamie and I always wondered what would have happened if they had been given both. I mean, it is a big problem deciding which you like best. And obviously you eat what is best, last. Although Jamie and I did have one friend who ate best things first.

You could almost go as far as to say, that the decision between raspberries and strawberries is a lifelong problem. I can never make up my mind about it until I am actually eating either, and then I know that whichever I am eating is my favourite.

We ate enormous teas in Scotland. Looking back on it, we don't know where it all went, because no one was especially fat. Perhaps we walked and ran it off, and the grown-ups must have talked it off. They talked more in those days, and were more interesting. Or is that the sense memory playing tricks again? I doubt if conversation has much to do with the senses.

The crunch of the car wheels on our gravelly drive, brought the tennis parties to a conclusion. The departing guests circled the driveway in front of the house because that was the way they had to go. As each car slid past the front door, the profiles of the guests changed expression. The expressions changed because the day was over, and they were heading towards evening and thoughts of a different day.

After they had gone, the fancy took some time to return

75

to normal, and sometimes it did not manage it until the next day when the Manse had slept on it.

Mostly, Jamie and I liked having the visitors because it helped to emphasize the fact of how nice the house was without them.

'You must try to enjoy your guests,' mother would say to us. But it was the very fact of 'trying' to enjoy them that upset us. We felt that either you enjoyed people or you did not. Trying was hopeless. But none of this mattered with mother because we knew, although she would never admit it, that she was quite indifferent to their comings and goings herself.

On the other hand, father thought they were fun. Probably this is because he made them fun, and quite often funny.

At the end of each social occasion, there would be a natural drifting towards father's study where the cool serenity of the room disposed of the hot day.

The carpet in father's study was old and worn, but there was a tiny, imprinted pattern on it which seemed to lead through to the lawn outside where the daisies repeated the design.

Looking out through the french windows, which we always did in summer because they were open and the chairs faced that way, we could see on to the glebe and then the river beyond. There was a white iron gate leading through on to the glebe and opposite the gate, on two hillocks stood the sentinels to our glebe. These beech trees were ancient and tall and their greatest affinity seemed to be with the sky. Although, at their base, the rabbit burrows were dug in at the infinitely sprawling roots, and Jamie and I felt at one with rabbits that would choose such a place.

Looking out from father's study we could see the Kirkcud-brightshire sky reflect, and then absorb, the vivid colours of evening. The gradual display of colour often appeared to start between the outstretched branches of these trees, and as the leaves turned black, the agonized brilliance from behind tortured each silhouette.

Even Oats was silent at this time of evening. He had no

76

desire either to hunt or pretend to hunt. He would sit at the bottom of the stone steps leading out from the study, and with partly closed eyes he would watch the dying antics of the beautiful sad butterflies whose lives would end as the sun went down.

'It is cruel that they should live for only one day,' I protested once to mother.

'But they don't know they are living for only one day. They don't know about our time. They live their time. And their time is a lifetime,' mother assured me.

Sometimes we would sit on right through the evening until every colour had been drained out of the ground. And just when all hope of seeing had gone, a great tangerine coloured ball would start to push its way up from behind what we called Midge Wood. By the time the ball was risen above the wood, it had become a huge translucent symbol of beauty, spreading over the world, great silvery pathways of light. Then the garden would take on a different look. Like memory, the moon cuts out detail, and we would be left with magnificent skeleton shapes, and long rich areas of darkness.

Ours were the only owls that I have heard that were neither frightening nor sad. We did not see them very often, but we heard them constantly, and we think they must have been happy in our woods.

There was a white one which used to fly straight across our vision as we sat in the study window, and we think it must have had an especial arrangement with the moon because it came to our garden when the moon was full. It is not possible to indulge in too much moongazing, because the deathrays are too strong, and the elevation to the world of immortality is too near madness to make it a proposition for any length of time.

Moffat did not go hunting on moonlight nights. Perhaps she did not like silvery mice, or she may have been afraid of the white owl. We think the white owl must have had a family near us because we went on having a white owl all the time we lived at the Manse.

Oats was less concerned about moonlight, although his own shadow upset him because he was too intelligent to think it was anything but himself. If we went for a walk on the glebe in the moonlight, neither of the animals would come, although, at dusk, both Oats and Moffat would accompany us.

Our rooks were the most affected by the moon because the treetop existence was too close for happy sleeping. The nests were always built at the top of the branches, and the delicate beech leaves are not much of a protection. Sometimes we used to think that the rooks were moonstruck because they would suddenly embark on a midnight raid to the other side of the river. It is not altogether surprising that the farmers got annoyed with father for regarding his rooks as private property. We told the farmers that we thought the rooks got a little moonstruck from time to time, but you could tell from their faces that they thought we had bewitched them a little. We knew that it was because any creature that had an association with father became personalized.

One of the things about memory is that it cuts out wet days. According to oneself, there were no wet days in youth. There was brilliant sun in the summer, and the winter was a Christmas card of pure snowy delight. But the senses, every now and again, can smell that rain. Galloway, when you can get rid of the poetic trimmings attached to remembering it, is a wet part of the world. In other words, when it rains it swamps and envelops everything and because it is such a contrast to the beauties of the scene when it is not raining, it becomes, in the senses, an even wetter part of the world.

Grey rain falling on grey water is the most depressing sight of the lot. Grey rain falling on brown earth, is better and grey rain falling on green earth can be quite good. But, of course, earth is not brown and grass is not green. Put on a green dress and go and stand in the middle of grass and you will see. Equally, try painting it using green. When it is raining, grass is greener than at any other time, but it is not green, as the rain knows all too well.

Occasionally the general sludge, mud and slush created by rain produce new colours in nature, and earth, water, and sky intermingle, swop colours and generally defy anyone to recognize what they are. This is when it is worth remembering rain, and it is this that one thinks of when the smell, sight, sound of it all suddenly returns.

Walking in the rain is quite good, but rowing in it is better. The boat which is sitting on water, becomes filled with water, and you, the person in it, then become enveloped and drenched in water. You can give yourself up to the whole, soaking, squelching sensation because, for once there is no counter-irritant. And, as the oars heave, not dip, in and out of the water, you take part in the magnificent movement that nature is going through at that time. You row faster and faster, or as fast as you can manage, and everything becomes a breathtaking, painful, saturated form of defiance. It takes days to get over it, and when you do you have probably got a cold.

But a few days in bed, with the smell of burning wood in the fireplace, eucalyptus on the pillow, bovril in the cup and clean linen on your bed, is really an additional pleasure.

Father quite enjoyed our illnesses, as opposed to his own, because he could victimize us with his books. He would go to the library in Castle Douglas and come back with his briefcase stuffed. Sometimes, after only half an hour's reading, he would return in to the room to know how we had enjoyed the book. If the cold was bad enough for our eyes to be running, he would read to us, and we liked that because he often cheated with the sentences. In the same way that he would embellish funny stories told to him by others, so he would embellish what he felt to be not quite good enough literature. After he had left the room, we would check, and the words would be different. In his head, father had a wonderful sense of literature. He was the most literate man I ever knew, but he would never commit anything to paper, not even his sermons. It is a pity about some of the sermons because we would like to have had them.

The other person to victimize us on these bedridden occasions was Mrs McSkimming.

Father fed our minds and Mrs McSkimming tried to over-feed our stomachs. Fridays were the worst because on Thursday evening Mrs McSkimming went to a Women's Rural Institute cooking demonstration in the school hall, and on Friday morning she tried out what she had learnt there.

It would be more accurate to say that the cooking demonstrations took the form of a baking competition. The housewives of the parish took it in turns to out-do each other in this particular art, and every now and again one or other of them arrived, either by error or by design, at a new way of creating an old idea.

So, out through the kitchen door, along the back corridors, into the main hall, up the stairs and finally to our bedrooms, would come the smell of baking. Following rapidly behind the smell would appear Mrs McSkimming herself, all scarlet and white. The white came from the flour she used for baking which she had spread up and down her arms and over her face. And the red came from a nature that was close to boiling point in any case.

The bedroom door would be flung open, and silhouetted in the doorway would be Mrs McSkimming's large frame, holding several hot manifestations of her labours, all dripping butter on to the bedroom carpet.

In order that the butter should not stain the carpet forever, and in order that Mrs McSkimming would not be reprimanded for trespassing out of her domain, we ate whatever she brought.

Jamie was usually sick because his stomach was less resilient than mine, and he was not so greedy. Only a very high fever prevented me from over-eating, and even when I was not hungry the smells coming from Mrs McSkimming's kitchen were enough to fire the imagination and ignite the digestive juices.

Mrs McSkimming had only one idea of how to cure all ills, feed the patient. According to her, if you fed a cold it would be unnecessary to starve a fever.

80

From our bedroom windows we could see the delivery men as they arrived in their vans. They all, always, stopped at exactly the same spot, twenty yards from the kitchen door, and at the end of a thin, mossy path that led from it.

Mrs McSkimming would waddle down to the vans, holding a large, white dish, and a little, wrinkled, brown purse. Mother and father never ran up accounts, and every-thing was paid for on the spot. The small, crinkly purse got passed from one to the other in the household, and, surprisingly, there was always just enough in it.

Mrs McSkimming's favourite delivery man was the fishmonger. He came in a pale, grey van, which seemed a suitable colour in connection with wet, cold fish, and his van always stood at the kitchen door for the longest amount of time. Jamie said that the fishmonger and Mrs Mc-Skimming were swopping stories, and he should have known because both he and his ears were flapping on those sort of occasions.

Sometimes Jamie would hide behind a high, beech hedge, which separated the washing line lawn from the path where Mrs McSkimming and the delivery men stood. It was not that Jamie was an eavesdropper by nature, it was just that he wanted to check on some of those stories. He had a good memory, and when Mrs McSkimming would relate the latest fishmonger tale to Jamie in the kitchen, Jamie would give the show away by saying, 'but what about the bit where the man . . . etc.' and then Mrs McSkimming would know that Jamie had been listening, and that she would have to tell the whole story.

Mrs McSkimming realized that Jamie did not understand what they were about, so relating the story did not worry her. Furthermore, she had no understanding of the main object of Jamie's enthusiasm. She did not realize that she was the best music-hall turn that we, or many others ever saw. Jamie and I only ever saw the same natural talent years later when watching the Crazy Gang perform for the amusement of each other, quite regardless of their audience.

Mrs McSkimming had father's gift of embellishing stories,

and Jamie assured me that when the story left the lips of the fishmonger it had only a remote relationship with the tale told by Mrs McSkimming later.

Today, for me, fish means Mrs McSkimming. And when it does not mean that, it means Jamie being Mrs McSkimming, and there are still moments when it is difficult to decide which memory one relishes most.

Cooked fish does not have the same effect, but with the sight of sodden scales, reflecting blue and green and purple lights, lying heavily on marble slabs, I am back seeing Mrs McSkimming as she comes up the path, supporting a heavy dish of fish, and a stomach full of silent convulsive laughter.

Meg did not have the same humour as Mrs McSkimming, hers was a little more subtle because she was a much wickeder girl. She was a taunting and delicious tease, and when Jamie brought home his first friend from Fettes, mother and father had to make a decision about sending either Meg or the friend away. Of course, it was not Meg that went, but in future she kept her flirting out of the Manse.

Meg had the type of sensuousness that helped those who spent any time with her to appreciate the luscious glory of being alive. She was the physical, peasant, natural counter-part of father. Whereas father tended to view life and all its magnificence, through the filtered accuracy of his mind, Meg felt and saw it all through her body.

Jamie and I used to go for bicycle rides with Meg when father and mother were out, and she took us to the sort of places where her natural appetites must have been given free rein on many occasion.

Bicycling into the woods, we watched the dripping sun-light as it came through the thickest part of the trees. And we enjoyed the succulent acquiescence of the wet moss as we pushed our bikes further and further into the shade. And when the tiny drops of light made only threadbare patterns amongst the trees we knew that we were near to the centre of the wood, and the black silence that Meg was after.

We lay on our backs on the moss, and lying as we did

near Meg, we felt the first stirrings of response within ourselves. The response to nature was very strong on those
occasions.

In the winter, we pushed our bikes into the woods over
crackling twigs and frozen mounds of earth. Sound is the
most important aspect in winter. Extreme cold is something
that can be heard because the air is full of electricity. The
crunch of our bicycles on the frozen ground sometimes
startled the semi-paralysed wild life, and there would be a
sudden, and momentary flash of movement.

Slanting across the branches of the slim, upright trees,
the pale sunlight of winter dipped its trailing fingers into
the middle reaches of the woods, and would then disappear
in tiny drops of phosphorescence amongst the icy grass
blades.

In the winter in those woods, there was nothing but the
beauty and the cold.

We never talked about this afterwards, and as we raced
home on our bicycles, we shouted at each other about other
things in order to see the breath spout out of our mouths in
defiance of the bitter air around us.

The last, long hill that led in to our village took the
speed from under our wheels and by the time we were
halfway down it, our bicycles and ourselves were out of
control. We had to shout to let people know that we were
coming, and as Jamie tore past me with his legs upbalanced
on the bar of his bike, I knew, even then, that nothing
would ever be quite so exciting for him again.

Meg always reached home first, because she was a Valkyrie
really, and she had two pairs of feet. One of the pairs was off
the ground and the other was on it. But the one on the
ground was the most earthy, pagan pair we ever saw.

We had an 'outside' woman who came to help with the
washing, and she of all the people, and animals, attached
to the Manse was the only one unbewitched.

She was ordinary, and nice, and always arrived on time.
She wasn't fat, and she wasn't thin, and we don't think
she had a face because we never had it in our minds. Oats

liked her a little, because at home in her small, immaculate cottage there was this fastidious little bitch whom Oats wanted to rape. We are not certain if he ever managed it, although once he did come back from the village with more than just a glow in his eye.

The thing about Mrs Gilcrist that has stuck in our senses for all time, is the fact that she had no fact. She is an entirely empty memory, but she serves as a resting ground for all the other much too acute sensations that surround her. Even the senses have to have a pause somewhere, and about Mrs Gilcrist there is no smell, feel, sound or vision. All of this is kept for the so much else amongst which we had to live.

CHAPTER TEN

A T THE beginning of Jamie's last year at prep school something happened to bring an entirely new element into our lives.

I had been a year at St Trinians and nothing had happened to alter my original opinion of the place.

There was a tyranny about the school that came from the very freedom we were given. It is my view that the teachers were as disinterested in teaching as we were in being taught, because we were given work on Monday, and so long as it was finished by Friday, it didn't seem to matter when, or how, we did it.

As I was only nine when I went there, my ability to organize and plan my working week was not very marked. So, instead of embarking on an educational career of great individual merit, I merely indulged in a system of radiation which kept me spiritually, and mentally, at my natural home, which was the Manse.

I wonder why Ronald Searle decided to depict St Trinians. It is possible that first he made up his own image of the all-time classic idea of a girls' public school and stuck it on to St Trinians. Or it is possible that he was drawing from live material. In which case, which live material? I wish I knew. But if I had had his sense of humour at that time, it would not have been necessary to do what I did. If I could have caricatured the place for myself I would not have been forced to shut myself off from it. However, St Trinians did do two things for me which have been invaluable since.

It gave me my first lesson in how to 'shut off'. Just, literally that. This is a form of mental invisibility, and it is a two-way process. You can't get out, and no one can get in.

The other thing that St Trinians did for me was to teach me to think in picture form. It was a necessity really. I had to concentrate on turning my home into a visual fact around me in order to cancel out the encasement of a place I loathed. It made life difficult because I hardly knew the difference between reality and fantasy.

It is possible that the other girls thought I was potty. I certainly thought they were. The fact that Jamie treated me more as a brother than as a sister did not help. It made me shy of girls and I felt that neither the girls nor the mistresses liked me. This did not even provide a feeling of importance. It provided nothing. It merely made me miserable until I learnt about the process of shutting off.

'Never, never underestimate the capacity of the mind, and the virility of the imagination,' father had said to us. 'There is a lifetime of potentialities stored up in there. Use it.'

So I used it for developing the imagination when I should have been developing the brain.

The bastion of my independence from the turreted splendour of this female prison was an isolated attic several passages away from the main body of the school. In there I dreamed, and in there I further developed the introspection that had begun during my period of illness. The only redeeming thing about it was that it was not so much an examination of my own thoughts as it was a concentration on the meaning of beauty. And beauty to me at that time was the Manse.

I made a research into the scenes and incidents of importance to my own life. And I made mental canvasses of all that I had seen.

It usually began with total concentration on the 'blue' of father's study. From there it led, almost inevitably, to the two most significant areas in the house for me.

The dining-room was a wide, mahogany room with

big windows and a high ceiling. Everything about the room gave the impression of space, and because we did nothing in there except eat, there was always room for thinking.

In one corner of the room there was a high-backed yellow chair that served no purpose other than to provide the bottom of a frame for the picture out of the window. There was a view from this particular window that put the Galloway hills into the middle of the vision. And because they were placed as they were, they sat on top of the yellow chair. No one ever moved this chair, and because of this secret communion that existed between the foreground, which we had arranged, and the background, which nature had arranged, we had our own manifestation of the word Art.

The other place of significance was the bathroom, where a red velvet chair sat snugly against the hot water tank. Everything about the bathroom was warm and comfortable and most of the conferences that were not 'study' matters took place in there.

When Oats was alive, and when he was not in the village, or out on the Glebe, he was on the red velvet chair waiting so that he could be part of the next conference.

What was the reason for the especial selection of these two visions? Father explained it to me ultimately.

One, the yellow chair, represented a spiritual need, almost a fulfilment, and the other, the red chair, represented a physical one. Those colours, minus the objects, mean just the same to me today.

But it was the event in the train, when mother was taking us both to school at the beginning of Jamie's last year at prep school, that got me out of that bad period of introspection.

We were travelling to Moffat in the train from Dumfries. We sat in a row. Mother was in the middle, and Jamie and I sat hugging the window seats in an effort to halt the all too rapidly passing scene.

Halfway through the journey, Jamie and I realized that mother was strangely absorbed with something other than ourselves.

Concentrating for a moment, we saw that mother had abandoned her modest approach to things in order to stare at the woman opposite her. The woman was startlingly beautiful. But beautiful and sad.

'Why?' mother was wondering to herself. And then she saw that the elegant lady had a young boy with her, and that he was wearing the same school uniform as Jamie. 'Perhaps that is the reason,' she thought. 'He is going to St Ninian's,' she said to herself.

'Is he?' she suddenly asked the woman.

A thin veil came up over the immaculate face, and sliding back from whichever district of thought that had retained her, the lady inclined her head in agreement.

Jamie swung his legs back and forth in an attempt to catch the eye of the boy, and when a very pronounced dimple appeared on a visibly altering cheek, he knew that he had succeeded.

'We come from the Argentine,' was the surprising remark from the woman, 'and our name is McEwan.'

Jamie giggled, and mother leant forward to the woman as if she was trying to settle something out of court. When there was no further explanation of this strange combination of name and place, mother asked the obvious.

'You have decided to send your son to school in Scotland then?'

'This is his first time away from home,' the rich and only slightly unEnglish voice replied. 'And I am afraid that I must leave him here and return to the Argentine.'

'Oh, how heart breaking,' was mother's reply. 'He must come to us in the holidays.'

There it was. It had been said, and nothing could unsay it. Jamie stopped swinging his legs, and tried to do the very reverse of attracting attention. He was appalled by mother's suggestion, and was working out how best to be beastly to the newcomer at school. Anything to stop him from coming to the Manse in the holidays.

It is difficult to be certain at what moment I decided that I wanted the boy to come to us in the holidays. It may have been when I saw the dimple. It may have been when I heard the word Argentine. It may have been when Jen looked at me with a long slow smile. When we got out of the train, and were alone, Jamie and I indulged in one of the rows that we brought about from time to time in order to let off steam. But on this occasion the row was genuine and rather urgent.

'Wait and see,' mother warned us. 'Wait until you have been one term with him at school and I think you will find that you want him to come to us for the holidays.'

During that term, I waited. And from a distance, mother watched. Father had been told about it, and he wondered.

Five days before the end of term, Jamie wrote:

Dear Mum and Dad,

I am bringing home a friend of mine for the holidays. His parents live in the Argentine. It is too far for him to go. You will like him. I do.

Love,
Jamie.

It was his decision to bring Jen home, and no one ever let him think it wasn't.

CHAPTER ELEVEN

W HAT DECIDED you to bring him, Fish?' I asked Jamie during the first moment that we had to ourselves at the start of the next holidays.

'Money,' was Jamie's surprising reply. 'We had a bet and I lost.'

'It's a funny way of going on,' I said.

'It doesn't matter,' Jamie replied, 'Jen doesn't mind about anything like that.'

Jen didn't. When he first came to us, he didn't seem to mind about anything at all. We were not particularly nice to him because we did not want him there, Jamie ignored him and I was slightly rude although I think it was because I wanted him to notice me.

Father took us into his study and painted a vivid picture of what it would be like for either of us if we were suddenly left on our own in a place like Buenos Aires. How would you feel if we were Jen in reverse?

We came out of father's study ashamed of ourselves and acutely saddened for Jen.

But Jen was not interested in either our patronage or our compassion. He was barely interested in us. But in spite of this he became a part of us. Jamie and I were such a close unit that had we been told that anything or anyone could intrude we would not have believed it. But the point about Jen was that he did not intrude. He never imposed himself on anything. If he had a need of anything he simply assimilated.

In time, he liked us, equally, and we loved him. We found that being with him was like looking at the whole of life through a magnifying glass. He noticed everything. From my point of view he was the perfect person to weed out introspection. There wasn't time for it, life held too much.

Jen was the same age as Jamie, but there were moments when we thought he must have lived for ever. It was not that he knew so much, it was more that he could both see and understand a lot that escaped us. He had a strange sense of the inevitability about things. There were moods when we couldn't get near him. He would go by himself and sit with the river and the life that was going on around it. These were not periods of deep, brooding introspection. They were times of extreme concentration. Sometimes Jamie got impatient with the moods and went off on his own. I never got impatient because I preferred his moods to my own. In any case, I loved him, and thought him beautiful. It is almost certain he was beautiful. And I thought him sad, and it is almost certain that he was sad.

'He is not sad,' Jamie said.

But father understood it. 'It is the last mysterious layer in the self that can never really be touched,' he quoted. And he knew that in Jen it was more untouchable and mysterious than in most.

If Jen needed anyone it was father. The ancient almost hopeless self in Jen needed the vitality and enthusiasm of father. They talked together for hours and father tried to put it to Jen that the quantum of beauty around him had a permanence. Such beauty saddened Jen because he knew it must go.

Jen was always the first to see things. He found the first snowdrop in winter, and then the daffodil in spring.

One morning he came rushing into my bedroom and said, 'Come quickly.'

We raced downstairs, out through the front door, along the drive, and up under the beech trees. Then he crouched down, and very carefully he lifted some leaves to reveal a fairy ring of toadstools.

'Alice in Wonderland,' he said. 'I wonder if the cater-pillar is here.'

I looked at his face, and it was radiant.

Early on in that first holiday I discovered that Jen was musical. Very acutely so. He heard it in everything.

How does music rank in the memory of the senses? Near the top, I think, because it is closely connected with the mind. Smell, taste, feel are sensations that can be re-lived almost exclusively through the body. But sight and sound are a little more complex. Perhaps there is no such thing as the actual memory of sight. By the time you have dug into the subconscious and reproduced it for the conscious mind the picture is altered. Sound keeps a continuous grip on the mind and provides a continuity with the senses. Music is always with you. It certainly was with Jen.

'Music is best in the morning,' Jen said. He meant the sounds of nature and their connection with music.

Sometimes in the early morning, when no one else was about, Jen and I would creep down to the river.

'Listen,' he would say. 'A chorus is made up of many individual notes.'

Later on in the same day he would pick out these notes on mother's piano. I think Jen must have had perfect pitch. And if that can be related to having a perfect place in nature, then Jen had it. Sometimes I try to remember the inperfections about Jen, but they have all gone. Were they ever there?

Every summer, as far back as we could remember, Jamie and I had gone with father and mother to Ireland. Grandfather had left his house by the Mourne Mountains to his youngest son because his youngest son was the only one who, grandfather knew, would never make any money.

We loved it in Mourne and it was natural that when Jen was with us, we should take him there. We took him the summer after his arrival with us and this is where Jen was happiest.

We caught the 'paddy', the London to Stranraer train, which made a surprising and dramatic halt at our little station nightly. Every night it went through the village at about 3 o'clock, and coming when it did, it folded the night in two.

We got to Stranraer at five in the morning and were on to the boat and moving towards Ireland by six o'clock.

The seagulls that hovered, and then plunged, around us intercepted the golden shafts, and the patterns that moved around us increased our already developing sense of excitement.

It was always exciting going to Ireland. It still is. The atmosphere, or to us 'fancy', of Ireland is what every child is looking for. It is not quite real. Or at any rate it has its own reality and this has nothing to do with any place else. The Irish do not take themselves too seriously because somewhere, at the back of their minds, they have the idea that the whole thing may be a joke. The Irish can be very annoying when they are outside Ireland, but they have created a wonderful atmosphere in their own country.

That summer the sky was very high and distant and there was nothing to disturb the vivid intensity of the land. As we sailed towards Ireland the sea began a reflection of the green that belongs, and has its existence, in only one island in this world. Jen watched it all through the water and when he lifted his head and saw it repeated again in front of him we knew that he was right in the middle of happiness.

The mountains of Mourne which 'sweep down to the sea', do so through our garden. On bad days they stand as bold, purple sentinels at the back of our house. On balmy, summer days they merge into the other shapes that make up the Emerald Isle. The year that we took Jen there, the mountains stood back from the scene and became a part of our lives only when we wanted that it should be so.

If you can swim in the Irish Sea, you can do anything. If you can swim and enjoy it, bathing anywhere else in the world will mean nothing from then on. It is a blissful agony. It is breathtaking and painful. It is utterly sensuous because at the time you can think and feel nothing else. When you come out you feel as if you have climbed Mount Everest and seen God. People look beautiful when they come out of the water by the Mourne Mountains, and the most beautiful person ever to come out of those waters was Jen.

In our family it was a matter of pride and honour to be

93

able to swim by the time you were seven. In the same way, we all had to scale Slieve Binian, the highest mountain in the range, by the time we were nine.

When we took Jen to Ireland he was nearly thirteen and he did all of these things with a fever and an ecstacy that heightened the pleasure for us.

Jamie and I had many cousins, and when we had Jen with us, there were only two that we chose for company. Then the five of us would take an all-day picnic into the mountains, and it was in there that we first learnt the meaning of losing identity. Looking back on it, Jamie and I feel that Jen knew about this before we met him. It was this that made him different from us. We had always been very much inside ourselves, and concerned, therefore, with the present and living moment. Jen's sense of assimilation which was something much beyond himself, gave him both the meaning and despair of his life.

Our housekeeper may have been right when she said that the Little People lived among the mountains.

There was one particular area known as the Silent Valley that acted as a magnet to us. It is possible that if it had been called Devil's Leap, or Rocky Gorge, or the like, it would have had no significance for us. As it was, we could not keep away.

It was no place for human voices because the echoes were a distortion of human sound. When we walked, we walked in silence, and our crunching feet gave out the only sound. There are no trees or bushes on the Mourne Mountains, and there are no birds. Occasionally, the distant call of the water birds can be heard, but they do not break the silence, they merely frame the void.

The Silent Valley is a place for thinking, and each of us have gone back and back to it, individually, and together, for that purpose.

Our housekeeper, Annie, was supposed to be the second-best witch in Northern Ireland.

On the whole, father did not go in for second-bests of anything. But over this he was thankful for a down-grade. Even as it was, we had all of father's family, which amounted

94

to about thirty cousins for us, coming to see us, with a view to getting at Annie.

After tea, because they always came for tea, they would slip into the kitchen, cross Annie's palm with silver, and the fortune-telling would begin.

In theory, father did not know about this barbaric sport. In practice, he was in league with Annie. Any tiresome member of the family was given the type of fortune that would not bring them back a second time. Father's surprised dismay when he heard what Annie had told them, was touching to behold.

Every night, Annie put saucers of milk outside the back door for the Little People and every morning the milk had gone. Annie kept one donkey, eight hens, two goats and, usually, about six cats. As none of them were ever locked in, it is certain that it was they who took the milk. But Annie insisted that the Little People came down from the mountains for it.

The donkey was called Mackawee, and he was not quite a donkey because he never managed to bray. He got as far as the intaking, upward note that heralds the whole blast-off, and then he would get stuck. Everyone said that Annie had bewitched him, and certainly he seemed bewitched on account of his human behaviour. He liked to come with us on most outings, but especially he liked picnics on the beach. When we played gramophone records, which we did, especially when Jen was there, Mackawee stuck his head in through the sitting-room window to listen. If visitors came to the house, the sort that had not been there before, they were confused to find that their every move was observed by a large grey head sticking in through the window. Our fear was that one day Mackawee would discover how to bray whilst in that very position.

During the months that we were in Ireland, father never removed his dog collar.

'Take it off,' we would say. 'You can't relax with that thing on.'

'Relaxing is nothing to do with a collar,' father would

say, and apart from swimming, the collar remained on.

One year we took him to Belfast and bought him a collar and tie.

'You look awful,' mother said, and the trouble was that he did.

In his heart, father had the feeling that clergymen were never really off-duty. Not that father was the sort of clergyman that needed to be dressed up to remind himself of this fact, He was happy in his 'dog collar', it suited him, and he was wrong in anything else.

'What about wartime,' Jamie asked him, 'you took it off then.'

'Not to relax,' father replied. 'It was to do another type of job.'

'Is being a clergyman a job?' Jamie asked.

I knew what he meant by that question. In a strange way we thought of father as having been born to become a clergyman. In the same way that he might have been born to become a king, or a duke. For this reason we looked on it more as a vocation than a job.

'Yes, it is a job,' father said. 'Nearly all jobs are service of one sort or another.'

'I suppose your boss is God?' Jamie persisted. 'Jolly nice, he is not too near you.'

'Isn't he?' father said with a smile. 'I think he is nearer than any other boss, in any other sphere. Unlike some bosses, who can have the wool pulled over their eyes, or can be fooled, this is one you cannot delude.'

The year that Jen came to Ireland was the year that we were overrun by rats and mice. It developed into a nightmare because the ordinary poison and traps proved totally ineffectual. Jen discovered the truth about what was happening.

Jen's bedroom faced the sea, and sometimes at night when he did not sleep well, he would get up and sit by the window.

On moonlight nights the silver path from the moon to our front door was a frightening invitation to someone whose thoughts belonged more in the cosmos than in

96

himself. The black and white world of the moon has a way of cutting out detail, as in a photograph negative, and it puts into high relief the startling clarity of that which you want to see. Jen wanted to see the sea, and the sky, and the worlds beyond the world of it all, and he wanted to feel the tiny significance of himself in relationship to it.

One night when the pull was stronger than usual, he crept out of his room, and when telling us about it later, he said he did not remember what he was going to do, he went slowly down the stairs and as he did so, he heard a noise in the back regions of the house.

One of the things about Jen was that he had no fear of the dark, or of the night. He was part of it, and it was in him.

He followed the noise through into the kitchen, and from there into the back kitchen. What he saw, made him stop where he was because he became conscious of trespassing into the private world of someone else.

Annie was feeding the rats and mice, and as she fed them, she released the traps that has been set for them. For a moment, Jen wondered if the moon had struck them both, but when he saw the expression on Annie's face, he knew that this was an act of love between one creature and another. Animals, people, fairies, spirits had equal significance in Annie's life. The miracle of the mind and of the body were a huge conception to Annie. God, her Catholic God, had created all creatures, all thought, all spirits, and there were equal rights amongst such beings.

'Don't tell the others,' she said to Jen. 'They wouldn't understand.' In saying this, she included Jen in the community of the enlightened few who knew.

Jen didn't tell us about this until many years later, but in the meantime something did happen about the rats because they stopped requisitioning our house.

'What has happened?' Mother asked Annie.

'They have moved on,' was all Annie said.

Only once was our peace seriously disturbed in Mourne. A car and a caravan came in through the driveway one day, and out of the car got Jamie and Jen's housemaster. Jamie told me afterwards that the fancy altered the minute he saw the man get out of the car.

He and another master had come to Ireland for the first time, and were going on a tour. They thought it would be pleasant to park the caravan with us for a few days while they 'did' the Mourne Mountains. We thought that the idea of them being there was a negation of living.

But because mother was polite, father potentially interested in everyone, and Jamie and Jen pupils of these individuals, the caravan was allowed to stay.

On the first day at about teatime, Mackawee gave the first intimation that all was not well with their visit.

'Does that donkey always stand there staring?' the elder of the masters asked.

'Always', we all said with emphasis.

The second day at roughly the same time, Annie burst in to the dining-room where we were having tea and announced, 'Excuse me, M'm, but the goat is eating your knickers.'

Thoughts if they could be X-rayed and put on view immediately would be worth every minute of any conversation ever heard.

At that moment thoughts were such a jumble that it is doubtful if any X-ray equipment could have coped.

Father thought, 'Good for Annie, she has scored a bulls-eye this time.'

Mother thought, 'I wonder how much of the knickers the goat has eaten.'

Jamie and I thought, 'Good, I hope the goat is sick,' because we didn't like the goat.

And the schoolmasters thought, 'What sort of a mother is this to leave her knickers around in places where goats can eat them.'

Fortunately for us they did not wait much longer to find find out. The following morning saw their departure.

But somehow the spell of that summer was broken, and a few days later our visit to Ireland came to an end. A telegram arrived for Jen, followed by a long letter for mother and father. Jen was not to be allowed to finish his education in Britain. He was not to go on to Fettes with Jamie, instead he was to return to Buenos Aires to pick up the pieces.

There had been a 'crash', a financial crash, and Jen's father had toppled with it.

Jamie and I had never heard the expression before, and in our minds we saw a combination of the San Francisco earthquake and the sort of pile-up that could be created by the racing car drivers on the T.T. track in Northern Ireland.

To start with, none of us took in the real significance of the news. Crashes, southern continents, half-Latin parents, trips back over the sea, seemed an infinity of time away from Mourne where there 'is no joy but calm'. We could not pull ourselves out of the green, sleepy summer and hurtle into the disaster that was to alter Jen's life and make us miserable.

'You will come back, of course,' mother said in an attempt to keep the continuity going.

'Oh yes,' I said. 'You must spend your holidays with us always.' It was a cry from the heart because I had reached the stage when I could not envisage the idea of life without him.

Jamie was the most realistic because he said, 'I will save up and come out to see you in Buenos Aires.'

Both Jamie and father sensed that he would not be back. The Argentine was a long way off and none of us had the money to bridge the gap.

When it came time to say goodbye, there was a desperate finality about it. Jen never spoke, he just looked at us, and the huge hurt was in his eyes. As much as he belonged anywhere, he belonged with us.

And when, after he had gone, I heard father say to mother, 'Poor Jen, I hope this won't make him relinquish his small grip on the earth's surface,' I had that awful under-standing of what he meant.

We did not realize that it would take another tragedy, this time of a world-wide nature, to bring him back to Britain.

CHAPTER TWELVE

JAMIE SURPRISED us all by getting a scholarship to his public school, Fettes.

We had not thought of him as clever. We knew he was quick, enthusiastic and gay, but the idea that he might be a scholar had not entered anyone's head. Except, perhaps father's. Father recognized something in Jamie that was in himself. He recognized that when Jamie wanted something there could be a singlemindedness about him.

Some time before Jamie was due to sit the usual public school common entrance examination, father discovered that there was something Jamie wanted very much indeed. He wanted to spend a week at Lords when England was playing Australia.

Cricket is not the Scottish game. A sprinkling are interested but, generally speaking, it is soccer that holds the attention there. However, we were not a Scottish household and as both mother and father were keen enthusiasts, cricket was a foreground element in our lives. One of our uncles had played for Middlesex and everyone on mother's side of the family, male that is, was a member of the M.C.C. Automatically they were joined at birth, and automatically they became interested, and then obsessed by cricket. I was the only member of the family a little outside this enthusiasm because, in my heart, I was much more interested in what was going on at Wimbledon. Today during the summer months, Jamie and I have an agreement. I am allowed to bore him about tennis, so long as he is allowed to bore me about cricket. It works very well, because he spends all his free time at Lords, and I am at Wimbledon. When we are not doing this, we are talking to each other on the telephone about it. We both talk at the same time, and the wires get hot with, 'backhands, leg ons, forehands, and leg offs.' None of it matters, because no one else is involved. If there is ever a crossed line, we consider the intruder lucky to be getting the price of two games for one.

But Jamie carries the whole thing further than this. He sits in his spacious solicitor's office in Lincoln's Inn, looking out over the 'Fields' contemplating the assets of being known as a good 'family' solicitor, and listening at the same time to the test news on the wireless.

Don't get the idea that it is impossible to do two things at once. It is possible. You can dictate a letter into a tape recorder about Vendors and Surveyors and draft Contracts and draft Underleases, and you can also be listening with full attention, to the B.B.C. commentator as his voice reaches a crescendo of delight as the 'last man' has just scored a boundary.

Once father had assessed the possibilities in Jamie, he thought up a challenge. He spoke about it to mother, and, between them, they said to Jamie, 'if you can get a scholar ship to Fettes, we shall give you a week at Lords next summer.'

Our grandmother was brought into this, because mother thought that that was where Jamie should stay in London. Grandmother agreed happily because for her it might mean a reduction in school fees. Grandmother said that she would add to the inducement by offering Jamie theatres in the evenings.

Jamie worked for a scholarship and then sat it. Not only did he get the scholarship, but he came very high up on the list of those who had entered.

He went to London for what must have been one of the happiest weeks of his life, and when he came back he was grown up. He had won a scholarship, he was a public school boy, he had stayed in London, and he had been to Lords. There was not much else a man need do.

I saw the change in Jamie and knew that from then on

he would grow away from me. It never happened completely but, equally, things were never quite the same again.

Shortly after Jamie went to Fettes, I expelled myself from
St Trinians. The nightmare joke had gone on long enough,
so one day I packed my bags and went home. When mother,
in a half-hearted fashion approached the headmistress about
having me back, the answer was 'No'.

And, 'No', it was.

Grandmother then decided that I should go to school
in the South of England. Kilts, sporrans and tweed jackets
were pushed amongst the mothballs and I became encased
in dark stockings and navy blue clothes. In fact, I liked my
new school, Queen Annes, Caversham, and, ultimately,
became so over-adjusted that I finished as Head of my
House, and a school prefect.

Father was very proud of this, because he came once to
hear me read the lesson in Chapel, and he thought the
fact that I did not start with, 'Here beginneth the first verse
of the Second Chapter of the Gospel according to St Mark',
with the same sort of ending, a very good idea. He wouldn't
believe me when I told him that it had happened because I
forgot.

'No, no,' he said. 'It was a much better idea just going
straight in to the passage like that. Much more dramatic,
much more literate, much more true.'

So I let him think that I was a clever girl, with many
original ideas. I was never a clever girl but I was always
full of ideas. Most of them were in the imagination and
most of them centred round Jen. I tried to steep myself
in school matters because this way I was able to fill up the
aching hollow in the middle of myself. When I wrote to
Jen I only let him know a quarter of what I was feeling,
although sometimes I did let it out to Jamie. Some of the
gayness went out of Jamie after Jen's departure, because,
to an extent, he felt we had lost Jen. Buenos Aires, the other
side of the world. Beyond the moon almost, and when,
eventually, Jen did return we discovered just how far away
he had been.

By 1938, the rumblings from across the water had begun. The deep, dark forebodings were vibrating through the surface pleasures of everyday life, and those that could, continued to ignore them. A few warned, and a few spoke in short, sharp words, but mainly there existed an atmosphere of placation. And placation won the day, and nearly lost freedom for Europe.

Eventually, the mad genius in charge of the storm-trooping millions went too far, and the Island Race was once again crusading for the freedom of all peoples.

All through the months of 'Shall we? Shan't we?' my history mistress at school was shouting at us, 'Why don't they put in Winston Churchill?'

Miss Lippet, our history mistress, was a liberal, and by that one meant that she thought liberally, but did not necessarily belong to a party. But, throughout, she had belonged to Winston Churchill's way of thinking and she concurred with every one of his 'liberal' thoughts.

When it came to the Abdication, she was wholeheartedly in favour of Churchill's thinking. We were never certain if she stood for Edward VIII, or if she stood for Winston Churchill standing for Edward VIII. At any rate, she indulged in what father called 'thinking with the emotions instead of with the mind'.

'What do you mean?' I asked him, because I did not like either Miss Lippet or Winston Churchill criticized.

'The monarchy,' father explained, 'is a system the British race employ to make things work both at home and abroad. It is a man-made construction to keep together an entire way of life. It is necessary to the British race.' And, in father's view at that time, the British race was necessary to the world. Therefore, at whatever price, the safe, good image of the monarchy must remain in order to hold that very system together.

'Edward VIII, unwittingly, is trying to destroy it. And Winston Churchill is supporting him because he believes in the Divine Right of Kings to act as they wish. This is emotional thinking and it is tied up with Churchill's sense of history, himself, the first Duke of Marlborough, and all the splendours of Blenheim. If he really stopped to think, he would find out that kings are manoeuvrable in the same way that Governments are.'

Father had nothing against Edward VIII personally, and it is almost certain he liked him very much. But to father, systems and processes were at work, and Edward VIII no longer was a part of the process.

When Winston Churchill became our wartime leader there was no one in keener support than father. All the brilliance, all the courage, all the determination was admired and cherished. And here, father considered, was an occasion when emotional thinking was not only excusable, but necessary. How else could the British people be made to struggle on in the face of absurd odds? Churchill's ability to muster the forces of determination and courage in each individual, had father speechless with awe.

'The poetry of the man is the thing that bewitches,' father said. 'The timing, and the magnificent use of words.' And then he added, with a smile, 'The almost amoral use of words.'

In the last war, father was too old to join up in the proper armed forces. If he had not been too old, it is almost certain he would have gone. As it was, he joined the Home Guard in 1939 as first of all a platoon commander, by 1941 he was a company commander, and then by 1942 he was appointed battalion commander. In 1942 he was also Vice-Convenor of the County, so sat on the Council's Emergency Committee.

By the time father became a battalion commander, Jamie was serving abroad as a subaltern in the King's Own Scottish Borderers, and I was working in the War Office in London.

Unhappily for Jamie, he was unable to witness something of his old nursery being turned into a Battalion H.Q. He was also unable to enjoy the sight of no less than four old-time Generals of Boer and Great War fame come sharply to attention to salute their small new Battalion Commander.

Mother and I were mystified by father's passion for military matters. And especially his passion for military history.

'It is strategy and the tactics side of the thing that absorbs him. It must be, 'mother reassured herself.

And, to an extent, we did need reassuring. Father's loathing of killing, in any shape or form, did not fit in with his obsession over military matters. But we realized, eventually, that the actual killing side of it did not feature in his mind. Pacifists recognize that man kills man, but will not have any part in it themselves. Father was not a pacifist because although he deplored the fact that man still wanted to kill man, he also knew that he was a part of the system and the process that made man want to do this. And, as such, he belonged.

He was anguished by the thought of the individual's misery and distress during war, but he was strangely fascinated by the movement of armies, and the planning behind them.

At any rate, he made a colourful and extremely efficient Home Guard Commander, and an invader would have been surprised by so much professional thinking.

I was able to come up from London for long weekends about every second month, and was able to watch the Manse change character outwardly, although inwardly it remained the same.

Day and night exercises were a great feature of the Home Guard during the height of the threatened invasion period, and as matters of war are not respecters of the Sabbath, father's dual role often used to reach a climax on Sunday.

He would go into the pulpit wearing battledress, over which the ministerial gowns would be slung, and mother lived through Sundays of doubt as to whether he would actually remember to put on the robes. Somehow, his short bulky figure looked ungainly in battledress, and the large head only seemed to increase the incongruity of the performance.

Each time that I heard the great, booted feet come up the steps from the vestry into the pulpit, I received a shock. The parishioners had got used to it, and knew that as soon as

Church was over, father would be off on some exercise. But I found the heavy feet strangely unsymbolic of father and his delicate approach to everything else in life.

Sometimes I wrote to Jamie about the state of the Manse.

'There is more than one pyramid now, Fish,' I told him. 'The large brown cupboard in the corner has been emptied of our old toys, and the first and original pyramid has gone in there.'

'I suppose the old generals found it a bit hard tripping their way into Battalion H.Q. over documents relating to maternity welfare, salvage co-ordination, deaf aids for the deaf and one or two old rocking horses,' Jamie wrote. And he was right of course, for all of that was still with us, as it was not until 1945, when father was elected Chairman of the Council, that he was given his own office in the County Buildings.

Jamie's old bedroom was turned into a dormitory for four evacuee boys from Glasgow. They had been bombed out of their home, if 'home' is the appropriate word for the slum they came from.

We had always heard that the Gorbals in Glasgow was one of the worst slum areas in the world, and judging by the ignorance and manners of our evacuees, this must have been right.

But, somehow, father managed to turn this visitation into something of an adventure.

The first morning after the arrival of the evacuees, mother went into 'their' bedroom to find what she thought was an empty room.

'Escaped,' she thought. But then she wondered to what.

Looking again she saw all four boys in one narrow bed, two top, two bottom.

'We were lonely,' was the explanation. Then mother realized that the huge dimension of a bed all to yourself could be frightening.

Father found a new fascination in teaching four people that life could be something of a gift instead of a struggling necessity. He told them a certain amount about God, because he discovered they had never heard of him except in terms of abuse. But he dwelt more on Christ because he was nearer and easier to understand.

'It is easy to believe in Him here,' James, their spokesman said. 'You have something to thank Him for.'

Father thought that that was a good point, and he used it several times in his sermons afterwards.

He tried to work it out for James and the others by suggesting to them that if they had known about God when they were in Glasgow, their slum, and their life in it, might not have seemed so bad.

'If you have got something to believe in that is greater than yourself, it gives a point to existence,' he told them.

I don't know how much of what father said they understood, but something must have been absorbed because when the war was over, they went back to Glasgow equipped with manners, a sense of appreciation, and minds that were open to the possibility that there might be something in religion. We heard later that all four did reasonably well with their lives.

Mother and I found James a fascinating study because underneath an almost barbaric exterior he had a natural elegance and humour. Like the others, when he first arrived, James thought nothing of wetting his bed nightly, picking his nose in public and eating with his fingers. And yet there was a grace about him, particularly the way he softened mother's heart over the bed-wetting.

Mother had taught them all to say prayers, and they did so each night, kneeling by their beds. Later on in the night they were made to suffer the indignity of being 'potted' in an effort to stop the bed-wetting. James invariably got out of bed with hands pressed close together and started to say the Lord's Prayer. It was a touching and pathetic sight, and he knew it.

Father tried not to show a preference but he couldn't quite resist James because James so often produced the sort of remarks that father could use again.

In the end, we were fond of them all, and when it came time for them to go I think there was sadness on both sides.

CHAPTER THIRTEEN

THE CURRENT of electricity that runs through the whole of existence, charging the many-sided interpretations of itself, gives to each person an extra boost now and again.

My boost came in 1941. I was sixteen then, and had just finished my last term at school.

It was late summer and the heavy, almost oppressive, feeling of dark green hung about in the air. Slicing the atmosphere with the front of my bicycle, I was rushing down the main street of Castle Douglas toward the lights and I was wearing a pair of jodhpurs and a bright yellow shirt. As I approached the lights they changed from orange to red, and waiting for them to turn green I turned my head to the left and saw a pair of long blue eyes looking at me.

I have thought since how strongly connected with colour the experience was. Since then every experience has come to me in terms of colour. I don't know if the thinking we do in the present is done in colour, but memory can conjure up tones that might seem an exaggeration on canvas.

At the time of this encounter I couldn't seem to attach the eyes to anything, and yet, something somersaulted inside me and I was breathless as I bicycled the four miles home.

The road from Castle Douglas to Claremichael is one of the few really straight roads you will find in Scotland. It is flat as well as straight and if you have the energy, the youth, and wish, you can develop a speed on a bicycle that gives the impression that the whole of life is rushing past you in the opposite direction. And as it goes, and as you go, you take off, once more, with Icarus wings.

When I opened the front door in answer to the bell that afternoon and saw Jen standing there I realized what was meant by the expression, 'my heart stopped beating'. This is, a spiritual fact and not a physical one. The truth is that for one moment in time, your time, everything stops. And into your mind comes all of the past, all of everything you have ever thought, and all of everything you have ever felt, and yet none of it measures up to what you are feeling at that moment.

When I saw Jen standing there, where he belonged, every second of time spent with him came back to me. Every microscopic detail and yet between opening the door and saying 'Hello, Jen' there can only have been a few seconds.

'Why didn't you recognize me in Castle Douglas?' was the first thing he said.

'I did,' I replied, 'but I didn't know you.'

And the marvellous thing about Jen was that he understood, exactly, what I meant. I had recognized him, but was running from the realization. By the time he arrived at the Manse, I was prepared to face the inevitable.

Mother and father were happy to see him. Our letters had continued throughout the years, but the contact had got more remote. The words were all there, and the exchange of news and happenings kept a veneer going. But what we all meant to each other was something that could not be expressed in letters because we were not certain how we meant it.

Once Jen was with us again everything was all right. The basic feelings had not changed.

Public schools in cold climates. Education in hot ones. Young boys in short trousers going to offices, going to brothels. Cricket and tennis on the one hand. Poverty and loneliness on the other. Each without relationship to the other, belonging only to itself. And yet, the carrion crow, or the vulture, who live off the defeat and destruction of others, also carry in their beaks, and in their claws, the seeds that grow.

The gentle meandering back through the years, and the swopping of tales in context to each other, came to an end with father's question, 'What are you going to do?'

'Join the R.A.F.' was Jen's immediate reply.

'You didn't have to come,' mother said and in her voice there was fear that we might lose him again.

But Jen didn't answer that, he knew it wasn't necessary. He must have known that we knew he would come.

What do you do with eyes like that, I wondered. There must be some way of protecting them. They have seen and absorbed so much already, and yet? Was it innocence that was there? It would be no good shutting eyes like that, the impressions would be projected from behind. What do you do, I wondered, what do you do with eyes like that?

After Jamie had gone, really gone, I had become talkative. When he was at home, I left the talking to him. He was better at it, and had more to say. After his departure, I felt that it was necessary to take his place and, as a result, may have become a nuisance to father and mother.

When Jen came back, I fell into silence again because he taught me about the silent way of communicating. He was reasonably expansive on anything to do with his life since we last saw him. But no discussion seemed necessary about the day in which we were involved. It was there to be lived.

Jen and I went everywhere on bicycles. Jamie's for him, and mine for me. He was going at the end of this period to start his training as a flyer. He had no interest in anything but being a pilot.

'I know it is going to be my answer,' he said.

'In what way?'

'Finding out about something.'

'You can't talk like that when you are off to fight a war. You can't talk about finding yourself, or finding out about anything else,'

'Don't forget,' he reminded me, 'that I have not been drafted, I have elected, more or less as a foreign citizen, to come and fight in this war.'

'For England?' I asked.

'Partly,' he said. But he would say no more.

There are parts of Galloway where you can travel for miles and see no sign of human life. Galloway consists of Kircudbrightshire and Wigtonshire, and the road from one to the other through the hills is a miracle of remoteness, and the road along by the coast, linking one to another, is a miracle of beauty. The earth and the sky, and the sea and the wind drive from your mind everything but what you see around you. On clear days the light is sharp enough to cut through to the sleeping areas of your brain. And the disturbance is exciting.

It was to the remote hill areas that Jen and I went on our bicycles, and when we reached a rounded summit, where nothing but the hills themselves could be seen, we would push our bikes amongst the heather and sit listening. Jen taught me to listen.

'Connect the vibrations of what you see with what you feel, and entirely new thoughts will come to you.'

To start with, I didn't do much more than think about Jen. I used to lie on my stomach staring at him, and wondering why it was that he was unselfconscious about my gaze.

'Is he used to admiration,' I wondered, 'or is he unaware of it?'

By this time Jen was nineteen. And the beauty had turned to a hard attraction. That is to say, it was hard in the sense that the face was chiselled and immobile. Set in a lasting cast of perfection. Only the eyes, which were framed by this sculptured mask, gave out the reason for such completion.

'That's what it is,' I thought to myself. 'He is complete. Then why the sadness?'

Sometimes I could not stand the silence and the almost nothingness of where we were and what we were doing. And when Jen was miles from me in his thoughts, I started to paint my first pictures. They were painted on mental canvasses, and were made up of about three colours. As there were so few objects to be seen, I learnt to make the most of the space between the objects, and in so doing discovered the marvellous unity that exists. That everything exists in relation to everything else, suddenly appeared to have meaning for me.

It was after this discovery that my true relationship with Jen began. I like to think of it as a slightly more adult one. Up until then I had tried to think of Jen and myself as a unit on our own, and I had done this because that was the way I wanted it. When I began the understanding that everything, not just two people towards each other, relates to everything else, I also understood that Jen, in particular would never belong to anyone. To start with, this realization was almost inacceptable. And it was inacceptable because I had decided that I would never belong to anyone but Jen. It's the kind of realization that can stunt you for life. When I discovered about the linking space between all objects, and Jen did this for me, I also discovered, that it is not necessary to have a total and exclusive relationship with anyone.

All of this type of thinking worked, and I could cope with it, so long as there was still Jen.

'Is the whole of creative art a form of self-explanation?' I asked Jen one day. We had come back from the hills and Jen was running his hand over the piano. Mother was sitting with her back to the window and father was facing it.

'It's a combining of the disturbances in nature with the disturbances in oneself,' Jen answered me.

Letting his left hand drift slowly up the keys, Jen said to father suddenly, 'I wonder if we ever think anything new?'

'There is a progression of thought,' father replied, 'that can be taken by a few, rare people to a point where it sparks off into an entirely new area. Yes,' father continued, as he searched his mind for the truth, 'I feel certain we are capable of new thought.'

'Do you see a hope for the human race?' Jen asked. It was the sort of question that seemed ironic during a period of international killing. But it was during just such a time that the question would bother Jen.

As we talked the summer day started to go down behind

the Galloway hills and we found ourselves looking at the copper light in the garden and breathing the only slightly altering air.

In the end Jen gave up his piano playing, and we sat for a time, motionless like a fresco.

The question had been 'Was there any hope for the human race?'

Out of the silence father said, 'I see a thin line of progress running through life. In spite of the individual horrors, there is now a feeling of public conscience. We no longer torture people if their religious beliefs do not coincide with our own. We do not sling the starving millions in to debtors prisons for stealing a loaf of bread, where they are left to rot and die. And we do look after the aged, the mental and the sick, irrespective of class and creed.'

'But none of this gives a point to existence,' Jen said.

Father thought for a moment. 'If man had the absolute conviction that the ultimate purpose of the universe was for evil, he could not go on. The knowledge would be too overwhelming. He would commit mass suicide, in that he would die off. Belief that he is helping to shape a better state of existence is one of the things that man lives by. The power of good which exists inside and outside of himself is his proof. And even although he may not relate this to a Divinity he still lives because he believes in this ultimate goodness, and he believes because he lives.'

We all sat, searching our minds as to how much of this was father, and what he wanted to believe, and how much of it was the belief of mankind.

'Surely,' father said into the silence, 'the proof of this lies in the fact that man is happy when he believes. And is unhappy when he does not.'

'The religious need is very strong,' Jen agreed. 'Otherwise there could not have been such massive slaughter in its name.'

'It is as well to remember,' father said, 'that people are not always rowing, or arguing, about what is really eating into them.'

'What do you think was behind most of the religious wars?' Jen asked.

'Greed and territorial ambitions, Fear, and lack of trust of the neighbours.'

'And the Crusades?'

'Romantic dreams dreamt up by people who would not attend to the proverty and misery in their own lands. And of course,' father added after a moment's pause, 'the remaining instinct in man, as opposed to woman, to go out and conquer, and fight, because of his feeling about his mate. Civilization will gradually curb this instinct, and other more altruistic ambitions will take its place.'

Dear father, he believed all this. He may be right. One day.

What upset me most about Jen's questioning was the fact that he seldom commented on father's answers. We don't know how much of what father said, Jen believed, or believed in. The proof that he was getting something from it, came from the fact that he always came back for more. And whatever else he believed about father, he believed that father was genuine.

Shortly after Jen joined his first air training station, I went to the War Office in London. Jamie was already fighting for his country. And it was halfway through Jen's air training that Jamie was sent home on sick leave. Jamie has never quite got over the fact that during the histrionics of the Italian landings he managed to contract anything so unmilitary as measles. To be sent home because of a child-hood illness seemed a little unglamorous.

I met Jamie in London and travelled with him to Scotland.

'Do you hate it all?' I asked.

'It's lousy,' he replied. 'It's even worse, it's endless.'

'Decent chaps with you?'

'Very.'

'Well that's something.'

'Oh yes, something.'

'We have got to win this war, I suppose?' I wanted them all home safe regardless of the victor. Love makes you selfish.

'God yes, we can't have the bloody Germans running everything.'

'It's all right then,' I said. 'Going on, I mean.'

'Of course.'

And that was about the last intimate conversation I had with him. For some years, that is.

By the time Jen was flying his bombers, I had changed my job. Sitting in the War House did not seem active enough so I had changed to become an ambulance driver. This amused father because he knew how bad my driving was, and he was impressed that I had bluffed my way in. I didn't tell him, because he liked the idea that we were exceptionable people, that I was there because of the shortage of drivers.

It was when I was attached to the military hospital at Tidworth that the news came.

I was sitting by myself in the cinema one evening when a notice was flashed across the screen. 'Would the duty driver report back to camp?'

Expecting to find myself on another emergency job, scraping some poor devil off the ground who had fallen parachuteless out of an aeroplane, I rushed back to the camp in my ambulance. As I walked in to the hall of our little F.A.N.Y. hut I saw father sitting in a chair.

'It is either Jamie or Jen,' I thought to myself. And then, even worse, it might be both?

Father greeted me with a sad, firm smile, and taking me by the arm he walked me out in to the black night.

He held on to my arm as we walked and then he told me that Jen had been killed. When he realized that I was not absorbing this huge fact, he just started to talk to me about many of the subjects that had mattered to us both in the past.

For some time we walked about in the dark, and then I took him towards the military hospital and showed him the various wards and offices, and then the garages that housed the ambulances. Father took especial interest in this, and when he had said all there was to say on the subject of viewing a military hospital at night, he began to talk about Jen again.

Father returned to Scotland the following day. A week later I took in what he had said. And because I could only cope with a part of it, I thought about some of the things father had said to me. 'The death of Jen is not quite so tragic as the death of many others, because, all through his life, he has been looking for the right reason for dying.' 'Had father been right?' I wondered.

Then I answered myself, 'But he loved life so, how could he live with the death wish.'

And then again I heard father's remark to me when he had said, 'Jen loved beauty, and he loved all he saw, but we are not certain that he loved living.'

On about his third bombing raid over Berlin, Jen's bomber had been shot down. His body was never recovered. And because he was never found his death has remained an unacceptable fact.

As time went on, I began to wonder about the reasons for Jen's death. I became convinced that it was not a point-less happening.

'Had he known? Did he try to save himself? What about the others in the bomber? Was he thinking of them?'

Finally, when I could not stand the questioning any longer I wrote to mother and said, 'I don't think I can live without knowing why Jen was killed.'

Mother wrote me back a sad but touching little letter full of her own strange humour. 'Darling,' she wrote, 'I am not omnipotent. I am unable to explain the workings of the Divine. But take comfort from the fact that Jen would have been amused by your question.'

That helped a bit, and I needed it, because I had got to the stage when I could not believe that other people were suffering the same with their losses.

As the months went on, my sense of loss about Jen got worse, and I felt that I could not do without him. And then I began the illusion that he was with me.

In the end, father had to deal with it for me. About

six months later, I was up at the Manse on leave, suffering from too many memories crowding in on me, when one afternoon father said to me, 'Why don't you come in to the study and talk to me?' I did not mind, because I had nothing to say to him.

Father was almost brutal. It was not often that he spoke in that tone of voice, but on this occasion he knew it was necessary. He said 'You must let him go, he does not belong here now.'

'But I am not sure I can do without him,' I protested.

'Walking about with ghosts makes one warped,' father replied with emphasis. 'You are beginning to look like a ghost yourself, and your attitude has become selfish.'

Disregarding the remark about selfishness, I said to father, 'Ghost is an appropriate word in a way because I often have the feeling that Jen was only on loan. I think he knew that he was here for a short time. Almost as if he were in the middle of something else. But if it is so,' I went on, 'what was the point of his coming at all? I mean, why did he have to embroil me?'

'Who embroiled whom?' father asked with a smile. 'If you cast your mind back you will remember that he asked nothing of you. You gave what you gave because you wanted to.'

'It was a selfish, one-sided arrangement,' I protested.

'On the contrary, Jen did a great deal for you. Remember it all, but let him go.'

As father talked, I thought about what he was saying, and I tried to decide if he was right. When he was finished, I went up to my room, and collected everything that Jen had given me. There were poems, scribbled compositions of music on the back of envelopes, books, and above all, letters. I took them, along with photographs of him, and locked them in a small case. I have never opened the case since. It is still with me, and locked.

CHAPTER FOURTEEN

WHERE WAST thou when I laid the foundations of the earth?'
Where indeed?

This was the sermon, or rather the text used for the sermon, by father, that stuck in my mind. Sticks in my mind. It is tied up with the other one, 'In the beginning was the Word . . .' because they both give the indication that before there was anything there was thought.

The book of Job was a favourite with father because it was both lyrical and perceptive.

'When the morning stars sang together, and all the sons of God shouted for joy,' is the sort of descriptive writing to which the mind and the imagination must respond.

In his sermon, father layed emphasis on the fact that the writer of the book of Job had an understanding of man's humility in the sight of God, which, several thousand years later, is sadly lacking.

It was unnecessary for us to believe that 'the Lord answered Job out of the whirlwind.' Almost certainly father did not believe it. But whirlwind is a symbolic force, as is any other force that surrounds us today. But father did believe in the writer of Job because, like Moses, he was a man capable of thinking up imaginative and forceful ways of putting across a point of view.

Living when he did, it is unlikely that Job had a knowledge of the Universe. Certainly not as we know it today. But he must have had some conception of the enormity of creation because there was humility in the question, 'Where wast thou when I laid the foundations of the earth?' It was a question he put to himself. It was something to be remembered during moments of self-inflation.

What were the stars to Job? What are they to us? What foundations have the stars? Are they crumbled and extinct? What remains after all of this? Thought?

To the fish, God is water. To the ant, God is earth. To man, God is the Universe. And to the Universe, what is God?

If you are seeking God, and according to Pascal this means you have already found him, it is not necessary to look as far as the Universe. Having appreciated the construction of one atom, and studied its function in the scheme of things, you have appreciated it all. That, at any rate, was father's view.

'Most of us are unable to analyse an atom, and nearly all of us are unable to understand its function,' Jen had said on one or two occasions.

The point that father was trying to make was that the Universe was in every atom. 'Wonder at the perfection of the smallest detail, and in so doing multiply the same thing a million times and you have got the whole.'

The first time that father, mother, Jamie and I were together at the Manse after the war, was the time when something strangely hostile came into the house. The something was brought in by a man who came to stay with us. What he brought was an atmosphere alien to the place.

As it happened, something good came out of it. This is often the case when contrasts are needed.

We think that Jamie had asked this man, Anthony, to stay. We are not certain about it as memory is dim, and the senses never came into it. At any rate Anthony had been with Jamie at one period during the war and Jamie must have said, 'Come and visit us in Scotland.' He may even have thought that father would be good for Anthony.

Anthony came, and with him came all the ignorance,

conceit, and prejudice that were given no breathing space in father's house.

Prejudice was an evil to father and he fought it as if it were an armed enemy.

Although the Germans had been the enemy in the war, father knew that theirs was not the only evil. He also understood, although it is something not readily acceptable, that to the Germans we were the enemy. And to God, we were members of the same family engaged in mortal battle.

'Death is not the only casualty of war,' father said often.

Father was prepared to listen to Anthony whilst he went through his war-time experiences. Father was interested in that, and especially hearing it from the inside. But shortly after father had given him his head, and he was launched into an uncalled for abuse of the entire German race, Anthony made his big mistake. Drawing in his breath, tilting back his head, and leaning with full strength on the back of the chair, he pronounced, 'We will have to watch the bastards in future, they are all rotten.'

Anthony thought that word, bastard, would get father. He said it on purpose, both to emphasize his point and to shock him.

Father was not shocked by the word, bastard, but he was deeply horrified by the prejudice. 'You are talking,' father said, 'of a race that produced Bach, Mozart, Beethoven, Heine, Goethe and Einstein.'

'They are either Jewish or dead,' Anthony said with emphasis.

Father looked at him and disbelief settled like a mask on his face. He leant towards the young man and said, 'It was also a German philosopher who said that in his view, "Man is unfinished and must be surpassed or completed".' And we knew that, at that moment, he was relating the theory to our guest.

I was angry with father and later said to Jamie, 'I thought that father was unnecessarily harsh with Anthony.'

'It was necessary,' Jamie said. 'That's the sort of chap who keeps wars and hatreds going.'

That night in bed I relived the conversation and father's sermon from the book of Job came back to me. And I realized that Anthony was the sort of person who would never hear 'the stars sing together in the morning', because he was under the impression that the Creation had begun with himself. And in realizing this I was able to give up the whole of my mind, and all of my senses, to the memory of Jen.

I managed to do this without distress, and Jamie who usually sensed what was going on in my mind, was able that same holiday to say to me, 'Fish, you lost your sense of humour where Jen was concerned, what happened to you?'

'I was in love.'

'It's happened before,' Jamie said, and I knew that he was saying it not out of unkindness, but to provoke more out of me, 'People have been in love before,' he continued. 'You thought you were doing something unique.'

'Jen was unique,' I defended myself.

'Possibly, but you lifted him so far above your head that you could not see him properly.'

'You don't know an awful lot about it because you were abroad during our adult years.'

'Your what!' Jamie exclaimed, and for a moment I was irritated by his smile.

'It was a very grown-up relationship,' I retaliated. 'You wouldn't understand, you were only ever light-hearted with Jen.'

Jamie's face changed expression, and he said, 'Now that just is not true. It is possible that I knew him better than you. Don't forget that when he was at school here I had him both term time and holidays.'

'What did you really think?' I asked Jamie.

'I think he was a little mad. And you are a little mad, so you got on. And,' he added suddenly, 'he was about the nicest person I ever knew.'

At that moment it was as if the curtains had been drawn back. The room was suddenly full of light and I looked at Jamie and felt bitterly ashamed of myself because I realized how much Jen meant to him. And yet I had behaved as if mine were a solitary grief.

'Father and Jen used to have the most amazing conversations,' I told Jamie.

'Yes, they would. They were near to each other.'

It was after Jamie had made this comment that I realized that he had understood about father's magic. And that he had known that Jen also had it.

Father and Jen were somewhere at the centre of things, travelling outwards. We are lucky that, for a time, we were attached to this journey.